Welcome to the wonderful world of Regency Romance!

For a free short story and to listen to the first chapter of all my other Regencies, please go to my website:

https://romancenovelsbyglrobinson.com

or use your phone with the following QR code:

Thank you!

GL Robinson

A Marriage Is Arranged

A Regency Romance By GL Robinson

©GL Robinson 2023. All Rights Reserved.

As always, in memory of my dear sister, Francine.

With thanks to my Beta Readers, who always tell me what they think.

And with special thanks to CS for his patient editing and technical help, and more especially, his friendship.

Cover art: GL Robinson, 2023

Chapter One

"Very well, Mama," said Louise Grey in her pleasant, low voice, "If I have been pledged to marry him, there's no more to be said."

But it seemed there was a great deal more to be said. Her Mama reiterated once again that the promise of marriage between her daughter and Gareth Wandsworth, the Earl of Shrewsbury, was of very long standing.

"Christopher, the present Earl's father, was your poor Papa's greatest friend at Eton and Oxford. They were constantly together and would have remained so, I'm sure, had it not been for his father sending him overseas to attend to the family's tea business in wherever it was...."

"China, I think, Mama," prompted her dutiful daughter.

"... Yes, China. A heathen place." Her mother shuddered.

Louise had heard this all before but she knew that once her mother had begun upon her interminable exposition there was no stopping her.

"Christopher came back to London to be married, and then both he and his wife went back to China. Your Papa told me he tried to convince his friend to stay in London, but it seems he had no choice but to go and oversee the family business. His father, the Earl, had suffered severe losses on the 'Change. To put it bluntly, they were dependent on the money from their tea business over there and could not trust the people on the spot. Rightly so, as it turned out.

"Your father and I were married a few years later. He and Christopher carried on as lively a correspondence as the distance would allow, and in due course his friend wrote that his wife had presented him with a son, Gareth. He must have been nearly seven years old by the time you were born. Your father immediately wrote proposing that you and Gareth be pledged to each other. His friend sent a delighted reply saying he thought that a wonderful way of cementing the friendship between the two families."

She stopped and took a breath. "Of course," she continued, "arranged marriages were more common then than now. In fact, the marriage that brought Christopher back from China was arranged. Your papa told me his friend had never seen the girl before their betrothal. From his letters, though, they seemed happy enough, and so will you be, my dear, if you put your mind to it."

She seemed to be waiting for an answer, so Louise dutifully replied, "Yes, Mama."

Her mother nodded with satisfaction. "Well, to finish the story, Gareth was sent back to England with his tutor when he was ready for Eton and the poor child never saw his parents again. They were both killed in an argument about something."

"Opium, I think, Mama," supplied her daughter.

"Yes, though what that has to do with tea I cannot imagine."

Since Louise did not wish to prolong the conversation, she said nothing. She had read about the history of trade between Britain and China for the last twenty-five years and the growing animosity between the two countries. The British public had an insatiable appetite for silks and tea, and a barter system had grown up, exchanging opium imported by the British from India for those commodities. There had been an article about it in *The Times* quite recently, warning of the Qing dynasty's opposition to the trade. The drug had caused problems in China from the start. She could have explained it, but chose not to, for her mother, she knew, was not really interested.

"When your poor dear Papa heard about his friend's death, he was cut up for weeks! He positively dwindled before our eyes! He was never the same afterwards."

The widow dabbed the corners of her eyes with a delicate lace handkerchief.

"I'm sure that contributed to his own death in the end! The sorrow must have weakened him. It's impossible that a paltry cold could have seen him off otherwise! So when the very last thing he asked me to do was to make sure you married the son of his old friend, what could I do but write to the family? We'd lost contact with them after Christopher died, but I looked them up in Debrett's and they were still at the same address. I thought they would be — it's been the family's place in London for generations."

Again, she seemed to be expecting some sort of a response, but Louise could add nothing to the old story. So she simply muttered something that sounded like acquiescence. But as she disentangled the long fringe of her mother's silk shawl from the legs of her chair, she wondered what on earth could have persuaded the Earl to even consider his father's pledge made all those years ago. Why on earth should he want to marry *her*?

Chapter Two

"Listen to what I'm saying, Gareth," said the older lady, her silver blond hair covered by a very becoming lace bonnet.

"I am listening, Gran," said Gareth Wandsworth, fourth Earl of Shrewsbury, sitting uncomfortably in a chair in his grandmother's elegant drawing room, his powerful legs thrust out in front of him, his heavy eyebrows pulled together in a frown, "just as I've listened to you on this subject often before. It's not that I don't want to marry, it's just that I can't find a woman I can bear to face at the breakfast table for the next fifty years!"

"I've told you before! Do not call me by that low name! And you mean not one of them can bear the idea of facing *you* over the breakfast table!" replied his granddam tartly. "If your grandfather hadn't been so idiotic as to die when he did, there might have been some hope for you. You've never been what anyone could call good-looking, but when you became the Earl every girl of marriageable age buzzed around you like a bee to a honeypot. Your response was to get on your high horse and glower at them, so it's no surprise they all backed away.

"Then your addiction to the low sport of boxing has made your shoulders too... too *large*. You look positively frightening! What a pity you didn't take up fencing! That's the sport for a gentleman! I said at the time you were far too young to be in control of your fortune. I suppose you couldn't help being the next Earl, but it's a pity you didn't learn to be a little more conciliating."

"But Gran…."

"Do NOT call me that! And you know perfectly well what I mean! I hear nothing of you but your association with That Woman and She Will Not Do! We need an heir produced by an acceptable woman. You surely don't want the title to go to Percy and his bloodless offspring."

Her grandson had a vision of his second cousin, a weak-willed individual whose slack, doughy body was sign enough of his lack of resolve. He had been snapped up by a sharp-faced woman a few years older than he. It was she who ruled both him and her timid son. If he inherited, it would be his wife who became Earl in all but name.

"Oh God." he muttered, "Anyone but Percy, or should I say Alicia?"

"Precisely. Find a sensible, well-bred young woman to be the mother of your sons, not Diane Courtland!"

"You know perfectly well I have no intention of marrying Diane, but I don't think any woman, well-bred or otherwise, could *guarantee* me sons," he retorted. Then he sighed. "The trouble is, the sensible, well-bred ones are all so dull! I swear I can hardly stay awake when I hear, *just so, my lord, of course, you are right my lord*, or, by way of a change, *I really couldn't say, my lord*. Doesn't a single one of them have an opinion on anything?"

"Of course not," replied his grandmother smartly. "They are not bred to have any opinion other than their father's and then their husband's. Besides, you alarm them too much with that scowl of yours. You have to find a woman who's not afraid of you."

But his lordship was tired of the same discussion they'd had many times before. "Look," he said, "if you really want me to marry one of this year's crop, put their names in a hat and pick one out. It's all the same to me. They are all equally lovely, equally accomplished, equally well-bred, and equally a dead bore. I promise I'll try not to frighten her."

"Don't be ridiculous! And if that's the way you feel about it, you may as well marry the girl your Papa pledged you to when she was born."

"What girl? What pledge?" The Earl sat up straight for the first time and looked at her intently. "This is the first I've heard about it!"

"I knew nothing of it either until I received a letter from the girl's mother the other day. That's why I asked you to come and see me."

She drew in her breath. "This is how it was. Your papa had a very good friend at Oxford, a Peter Grey. I remember him well. He came here often. A very pleasant, good-looking young man. In fact, your papa's chief objection to going to manage the family tea business in China was that that they wouldn't be able to run around together as they had been used to. But your grandfather needed him to go, and off he went.

"As you know, he came back to marry your mama, then returned to China, where you were born. What Peter Grey and he said to each other on that occasion I don't know, but when Grey subsequently married and his wife gave birth to a girl, they apparently exchanged letters agreeing that the two of you would be married. You were about seven at the time. It was just before you came home to go to Eton."

She stopped for a moment and put her lace handkerchief to her eyes. "But then, of course, your poor papa and mama were killed in that terrible way. We never knew the story, but it was something about payments and money. I could never forgive your grandfather for sending them there! Thank God you were already here! You would probably have perished too."

She was silent for a moment, lost in her memories, then continued. "Anyway, Grey's wife wrote to me quite recently to say her husband had passed away and telling me about the old promise. She has your Papa's letters agreeing to the match. The girl is eighteen now, but they couldn't bring her out while they were in black gloves and now they'll have to wait till the next season. In any case, it seems she's been away somewhere at school and cares nothing for society. According to her mama, she's very quiet and ladylike."

"Sounds perfect," said the Earl ironically. "Another dead bore. But she can't be any worse than the rest. Though," he said, as another idea struck him, "she may be a good deal better. If she cares nothing for society she won't mind staying at home building the nest while I go my own way, and if she's as well-bred as you think, she won't subject me to any scenes. I'll go to see her, and so long as she's passable, she may as well be the one."

He kissed his grandmother on the cheek and strode towards the door.

"If she'll have you, you mean," said his grandmother. But he was gone.

Chapter Three

The Earl had duly sent a letter to Mrs. Grey requesting an interview with her daughter. Receiving an answer in the affirmative, at the appointed time he presented himself at their home about twenty miles outside London.

It was a fine spring day and he rode his favorite hunter, a huge animal who tossed his glossy head and who no one but his lordship could control. Louise, looking surreptitiously from behind the long velvet drapes of the drawing room windows saw him arrive. She couldn't really see his face, but on horseback, straight-backed and effortlessly holding the spirited horse in check, a curly beaver hat on his head and a many-caped cloak over his broad shoulders, he looked immensely powerful.

The butler showed him into the drawing room a few minutes later, announcing sonorously, "The Earl of Shrewsbury, Madam."

Both mother and daughter rose. The Earl hesitated and then went to Mrs. Grey and bowed over her hand.

"Gareth Wandsworth, Ma'am," he said in a cold, hard voice. "You will forgive my riding attire, but I thought this interview had best be accomplished as rapidly as possible."

It was clear he had come on his horse because that's exactly what suited him. He wouldn't keep the animal waiting in the keen wind blowing that afternoon, and it gave him an excuse for a speedy departure. In other words, they were both being subjected to his rapid judgement. But after a first astonished glance at him, Louise kept her eyes lowered.

For the Earl of Shrewsbury literally took her breath away. He exuded an enormous sense of power. He looked as if he was sure of what he wanted, and equally sure he would get it. He was not overly tall, but his shoulders and chest were very broad. His tailor had done his best to confine them within the limits of his well-cut coat, but nothing could disguise the muscle beneath.

His general appearance was that of a perfect gentleman. His hair was swept forward into what she later learned was the classic Brutus cut made popular by Beau Brummel. His top boots, now somewhat dusty from the ride, were cut so close to his muscular legs, she wondered fleetingly how he got them off. But his few words on entering had already shown his manners were not good, and she had seen at once that he was not handsome. In fact his features were downright ugly. His complexion was swarthy and his very dark eyes were overhung by heavy eyebrows that almost met in the center. His hooked nose was the most prominent feature of his face, between lean cheeks with two lines that ran down to the sides of his narrow-lipped mouth and his decided chin. He looked almost angry.

Mrs. Grey sank into a curtsey and replied more graciously than the Earl's manners warranted.

"You are welcome here, my lord," she said, "no matter how you appear or how long you are able to stay."

Then rising, she said, "May I make my daughter, Louise Grey, known to you?"

She led him where Louise was standing. At his approach, her heart began beating so furiously she was sure both her companions could hear it. She curtseyed in such mental confusion she didn't know whether she had made it too shallow or too low. This nicety had been the object of much instruction at the Young Ladies'

Academy she had attended, but now, when she most needed them, the lessons deserted her.

She realized that nothing in her life had prepared her for this moment. She had been told repeatedly not to put herself forward, not to be unbecomingly bold, not to put her own desires first. As a result, she had never even asked herself what she really wanted. But suddenly, and with complete clarity, she knew. She wanted the Earl of Shrewsbury.

For his part, he beheld a woman with no style or beauty. She was too short and too thin. Her complexion was sallow, her neck too short and her brow too low. Her appearance was not aided by the tight braid that held her brown hair close to her head. Her ugly brown gown was lamentable. Even five years ago, it could never have been fashionable.

Louise's mother had urged her to wear something else. "You have the new sprigged muslin gown! It brings out the blue in your eyes. Don't you want him to see you looking your best?" she had cried when she had seen her daughter descending the stairs earlier in the afternoon. "Besides, it cost me all of twenty pounds. If now is not the occasion for wearing it, I don't know what is."

"No, mama, he should see me as I am. I would not want to mislead him. I am not a beauty, and it's best he know it."

"No, you are not a beauty," sighed her mother, "but you would look better if you would allow your hair to curl by your ears instead of wearing it in those tight bands!"

"I'm comfortable like this," said Louise quietly. "Anyway, it can't be for my looks that he wants me. In fact, I don't know why he wants me at all, except for that old promise, which he surely doesn't feel himself bound to!"

"He will want a sensible, well-bred girl," responded her mother, unconsciously echoing the Earl's grandmother. "And you are a perfect choice for that. You will know how to behave in society and you will not embarrass him with enacting Cheltenham tragedies if his attentions should happen to wander."

"I see," said Louise. And privately she thought, *I am to be the wife at home while he amuses himself elsewhere. How very convenient for him.*

Now faced with the man for whom this convenience was to be arranged, she made a decision. She wanted him and she would marry him. But she would be more than just a vessel for his children. It might be an arranged marriage, but she vowed there and then she would arrange it to suit herself. Her face, schooled by years of discipline, remained expressionless and plain, and although when something touched her ready sense of the ridiculous her mouth was inclined to turn up at the corners, it did not do so now. A pair of wide, intelligent blue-grey eyes was her only distinguishing feature. He caught a brief flash of them now, before she lowered her gaze.

There was a silence, then her mother said, "I shall leave you alone for a few minutes, if you don't mind. I find I have overlooked a direction to Cook. I shall return presently."

When the door clicked behind her mother, there was total silence. Finally, Louise found her voice.

"Won't you sit, my lord?" she said. "You must be tired after your ride, even on such a beautiful and obviously powerful horse."

"Oh, you saw Jupiter, did you?"

"Yes, I saw you arrive. He attracted my attention at once."

She turned her wide gaze upon him.

Was she challenging him, telling him she understood his plan of escape? It annoyed Gareth to be so transparent.

He was going to rebuff her. She was even worse than he had imagined. When her mother had left the room he had almost decided to make his excuses and leave too. Her mouse-like demeanor and drab appearance were more than he thought he could bear, even in a complaisant wife. But the expression in those grey eyes intrigued him, so he controlled himself and said instead, "No, it's best I stand for what I have to say, and perhaps for you to stand too."

Without further hesitation, he continued.

"I'm sure you know of the er... promise made between our fathers. They intended us to be married. I am here to tell you I am willing to honor that promise."

Louise wide gaze regarded him steadily.

"Thank you," she said. "I am conscious of the honor you do me and I gratefully accept your offer." She hesitated for a moment then said, "I promise you now that if our marriage is not a success, it will not be for lack of effort on my part."

If the second half of the answer surprised him, he dismissed it as that of a young woman unaccustomed to the conventions of society.

"In that case," he responded with a bow, "I believe convention requires me to reply you make me the happiest of men."

Convention may require it, but we both know that's a lie. The thought sprang immediately to her mind, and the corners of her mouth curled up in amusement at his obvious falsehood. Louise controlled herself and simply curtsied, holding out her hand.

The Earl saw the shadow of a smile and frowned. *Was this chit making fun of him?* But he bent over her hand, and straightening said, "I hope you will do me the honor of receiving me next week with my man of business. We will have settlements and er... details to discuss. I shall send you a note of the day and time."

As she inclined her head in acquiescence, the drawing room door opened and her mother came in.

"His lordship has offered for me, mama," said Louise baldly, "and I have accepted."

"Oh, my dear!" cried her mother. "Please allow me to congratulate you both. I wish you very happy!"

There being no effusive acclamation from either party, Mrs. Grey said, "I hope you will stay to dine with us, my lord. *En famille*, you know."

"I'm afraid I must decline. I'm expected for dinner in town," replied their guest. "And I don't care to leave my horse standing in the wind any longer."

He glanced at Louise, who again swallowed a smile. Now he was sure she was mocking him. Irritated, he bowed and, without a backward glance, left them.

Chapter Four

"Well, my dear! Didn't I say he would want to marry you?" cried her mother. "You are exactly the wife a man like him is looking for. You are well bred and you know not to make a fuss. But my goodness! One cannot call him good-looking. And his shoulders! He looks, well, he looks almost like an ape! Nor are his manners exactly what one expects from a gentleman. But then, he is probably accustomed to people toadying to him." She looked searchingly at her daughter. "I hope you did not find him altogether unappealing, my dear. I would never push you into marriage with a man you found repulsive."

"No, I did not find him repulsive."

She hesitated. How could she explain the irresistible pull she felt towards him? She knew he was ugly and unmannerly, but she couldn't help it.

"I must agree, though," she said with a light laugh, "we will make the ugliest couple in London. Our poor children will have to look further than their parents for any share of beauty. Let us hope they take after their grandmama!"

"Oh, my dear!" her mother smiled, "I can have no pretentions to beauty now, though it's true I was much admired when I was younger."

"Nonsense, Mama! You know you are still a very pretty lady. Everyone says so. I fear when I'm no longer here to frighten them off you will fall prey to hosts of suitors."

"Now you are being ridiculous! And you are not ugly! If you would only let your hair curl by your ears instead of putting it in those tight bands, you would look so much better!"

"But he offered for me as I was, with my braid and my old brown gown."

Since this was irrefutable, Mrs. Grey could not contradict her. But privately, she thought that after the wedding ceremony her daughter was going to have to do a little better if she wanted her husband to stay close to the hearth. He might be rude and look like an ape, but with his position and money there would always be women who found him attractive.

Her daughter knew what she was thinking but said nothing. She had promised their marriage would be successful, and she had meant it. She didn't know how yet, but she would arrange it.

The Earl returned the following week, having sent the promised note of the day and time of his arrival. On this occasion, he arrived in a carriage drawn by four beautiful bays. Entering the house, he ordered the butler to have them led to the stables. When informed of this by her startled manservant, Mrs. Grey was a little shocked at his presumption, but gratified that it at least showed his intention of staying for somewhat longer.

Louise knew he had been shown into the library where her mother was waiting. She stayed in her room until a footman came to inform her she was wanted. He delivered the message some twenty minutes later, and she descended the stairs slowly, again clad in her brown gown, her curly hair tightly held in its bands.

The gentlemen rose when she entered, and she saw a flash of surprise in the eyes of the gentleman who must be his lordship's man of business. She understood. She must look quite different from the fashionable women in London.

"Ah, Miss Grey, there you are." The Earl did not come forward to greet her, but gave a shallow bow from where he was standing.

He indicated his companion. "This is Arnold Booking, my man of business."

The solicitor, a grey-haired older man, did approach her; he bowed formally and murmured, "Miss Grey."

They sat at the long library table, on top of which a leather-covered box lay open, an inkwell and pen next to it. Mr. Booking pulled a chair out for Louise next to her mother. The Earl merely sat down.

"His lordship has been most generous," said Mrs. Grey.

She put a piece of paper in front of her daughter and Louise read it carefully. She had the impression her future husband was not expecting her to do so, for he drew his prominent eyebrows together in a frown. He said nothing but tapped his fingers on the polished surface of the desk. To her astonishment she saw that after her marriage she was to be given the enormous sum of a thousand pounds a quarter. This was ten times more than her current allowance.

However, she did not want to appear like an excited schoolgirl being given an unexpected treat. She nodded slightly in the Earl's direction and said, "Yes. I see. That will be satisfactory."

There was a moment of silence, then Mr. Booking said, "If you would both be so kind as to sign that you have read and agree to what is laid out here?"

The Earl reached for the pen and ink, signed the document in silence, then pushed it towards her. Under his signature, which was simply the word *Shrewsbury* written in a determined hand, her mother signed her name and added *for my daughter, Louise Mary Grey*. Mr. Booking had indicated that since Louise was not yet twenty-one, her mother would have to sign for her.

The solicitor produced a pounce box and shook fine sand over the signatures.

"Now," he said, looking a little anxiously at Louise's mother and herself, "we come to the more delicate issue of his lordship's, er, conjugal rights."

Louise couldn't stop herself. "Conjugal rights?" she said in astonishment.

"Yes," said the Earl, speaking for the first time since she had sat down, "I think it best for this to be laid out so there is no misunderstanding later. It is entirely usual in France where as far as arranged marriages are concerned, these things are managed better than here."

Apparently anxious to have done with this part of the settlements, the solicitor said quickly, "His lordship proposes once a fortnight until the first child is conceived and if it is a male child, once in every thirty day period thereafter, the actual days by mutual consent."

Louise looked at her mother, who, however, refused to meet her eye.

"You must forgive me," she said quietly, feeling a blush spreading over her cheeks, "I had not considered this question at all. I should like to speak to my mother in private, if you please."

The Earl drew his brows together, but after a hesitation he rose, followed by his man of business. They left the room.

"Mama! Have you ever heard of such a thing?" she said in an anxious semi-whisper.

"No-o," replied her mother slowly, in the same whisper, "but you know, my dear, it is a good idea. One is otherwise in the position of constantly wondering whether one's husband is, well, going to visit one that night. That can make for, er, disagreeable uncertainty. This way, you will agree and it will be done, and you will be free for two weeks until the next time. I think many women would like that. I know I would have. Not that I didn't care for your father's attentions, you understand," she added quickly. "But it will make your life more, well, more comfortable. You'll see."

"I suppose so," said Louise doubtfully, "Though since I know rather little of what is entailed, I cannot tell how I shall feel."

"Well, we can't go into all that now," said her mother hurriedly. "We cannot keep his lordship waiting. He didn't seem to want us to discuss it at all."

"I don't want to be difficult, mama, but at this point, his wishes concern me less than my own. Of course we cannot discuss it now, but please let us talk of it later."

Her mother looked even more uncomfortable but said, "Yes, yes, later, but not now."

Louise went to the library door and opened it. The two men were sitting next to each other on the straight-backed bench in the hall, for all the world like two schoolboys waiting to see the Dean. Louise's wide eyes danced with amusement at the thought.

Arnold Booking noticed them. *Why, she is not such a mouse as she appears,* he thought, *I wonder if Gary appreciates it.*

He always called the Earl *Gary* to himself. The man was so infernally superior, he liked to take him down a notch. The old Earl had been much easier to deal with. He smiled at Louise and she smiled back. *Yes, definitely not a mouse,* he decided.

They came back into the room. Once they were seated, Louise said calmly, "I agree to this … arrangement."

Her future husband merely nodded.

His man of business produced the document, which they both signed as before. Mrs. Grey invited the gentlemen to take a glass of sherry to celebrate the conclusion of their business.

"Yes, please do," said Louise quietly. "The horses are stabled, so there is no danger of their taking cold."

Dammit, thought the Earl. *Does the girl miss nothing?* But he bowed in acquiescence and accepted a glass of sherry. He was surprised when it turned out to be remarkably good.

Chapter Five

"Well, Gran," said the Earl, coming into the salon where his grandmother was dozing by the fire, "I must say, I thought you would be agog to know all about my pledged bride. Instead, I find you asleep."

"I was not sleep," said his grandmother, ignoring for once the appellation she found so disagreeable. She straightened her cap, which had slid forward over one eye. "I was merely resting a little. But don't tell me you made the girl an offer! Is she so pretty it was love at first sight?"

"No." said his lordship, "Not at all. Quite the opposite. She's too short, too thin, very plain and dresses appallingly. But she is a lady."

"Goodness! You say it's already all arranged between you?" His grandmother sat up straight in her chair.

"Yes, it's all arranged. I offered, she said yes and Booking and I went to see her with the Settlements and all that. Wasn't that what you wanted? Don't tell me it was all a hum!"

"Of course it wasn't a hum, you silly boy. I do want you to marry a nice girl. You said she was a lady, but she *is* a nice girl, at least? Even if she isn't pretty?"

Gareth hesitated. "I can't tell you. She didn't say much. I wasn't there long the first time. Then the second time I was with Booking, so there was no occasion for private communication."

"Whatever can you mean? Didn't you at least have a conversation with her?"

"No, there wasn't the least need. She accepted my proposal and that was that. I rode over and I didn't want to keep Jupiter waiting too long in the wind."

"You mean you rode over there deliberately on that overpriced thoroughbred of yours so that you'd have a good excuse to leave early! I declare, I'm ashamed of you, Gareth!"

"Why? You were the one who told me to ask her to be my wife. You didn't expect me to waste my time making love to her, did you? I told you, there wasn't the least need! She was perfectly willing."

"But a gentleman doesn't visit a woman he thinks he may marry already thinking of a rapid escape! If she had been a positive antidote, you could have made your excuses in an appropriate manner."

"She is almost a positive antidote! I can tell you when I first saw her, I was glad I'd kept the horse waiting outside. I nearly left again on the spot. But something made me go through with it. It's odd, but I had the suspicion she was laughing at me and I was damned if I'd let her get away with it. Then she said something rather strange when I offered for her. She said *I promise you now that if our marriage is not a success, it will not be for lack of effort on my part*. I've thought about that since, and I'm not sure what she meant by it."

"Laughing at you? Why should she do that? I'm surprised you didn't frighten her to death. And it seems evident what she meant! She wants the marriage to succeed. I think it handsome of her to say so much, especially as from what you've told me, you made no attempt to engage her at all!"

"What can that matter? We have our whole married life to get to know each other. And she wasn't afraid of me. Anyway, I'm no doubt refining on it too much. She has no experience of the world and it's unlikely she'd be subtle."

Chapter Six

The inexperienced, unsubtle girl was at that moment engaged in drawing a caricature of her future husband.

Louise had discovered a talent for this type of art while she was at school. She did these comical drawings for her own lively amusement and rarely showed them to anyone. She had an uncanny knack of being able focus unerringly on the aspect of her subject's physiognomy that, when exaggerated, made him or her appear ridiculous. Her drawings of unpopular teachers had once been discovered and shown around amongst the other girls at school, causing anger and recriminations. She had apologized, and thereafter vowed to keep them to herself.

Her mother entered her room just as she was finishing the caricature of the Earl of Shrewsbury. It exaggerated his large nose, lowering brow and ape-like shoulders. It was clearly recognizable as him; he looked both comical and slightly frightening.

"Oh, my dear!" exclaimed her mother, "You aren't still doing those unflattering drawings, are you? I hoped you had learned your lesson. Really, you shouldn't! Especially not of the Earl! It isn't proper to make fun of him in that manner."

Louise hastily shoved the drawing into a leather bound portfolio. "I didn't mean for anyone to see it. Don't scold me, mama. It amuses me and helps me to see things clearly. If I find myself thinking too much about a person, drawing a caricature helps to… to relieve my mind."

In fact, she was trying to convince herself there was nothing lovable in the person of the man who made her heart give that uncomfortable jump when she saw him.

"But why shouldn't you think about your fiancé? I'm sure his rather fierce and haughty appearance conceals a kind heart."

"Oh, Mama, you know you don't think that at all! I'm sure he looks fierce and haughty because he *is* fierce and haughty and has a bad temper besides! But it's not that, mama. I can deal with bad temper. It's the whole question of *conjugal rights*. It's worrying me. It must have worried you before you were married?"

"Well, yes, it did, but your father was a gentleman and it was perfectly fine in the end."

"Oh dear! I'm sorry to persist, mama, but what do you mean *in the end?* What about the beginning? What is he going to *do* exactly?" Then she added, looking down and blushing, "The girls at school had some idea about it being just like when you mate horses. The stallion puts his... *thing* in the mare's bottom! Is that it?"

Her mother looked embarrassed. "How you do take one up, Louise! And I find it very distasteful to discuss such matters. I'm shocked to think that was the tenor of the conversation amongst you young ladies!"

As Louise began to protest, she hurried on, "But since you ask so plainly, I shall answer you plainly. Yes, it is like a horse, but not your posterior, the other, er, opening in that, er region."

"You mean my...?"

"Yes, exactly."

"Oh."

There was a silence.

"But what about if I have my... my monthlies?"

"Well, of course, you don't do it *then*."

"But how will he know?"

"You'll tell him."

"You mean we have to talk about all *that*?"

"No, not exactly. You just give him a hint the first time and after that he'll be able to work it out."

"A *hint*? What sort of a hint? Anyway, how will I know if he wants to... you know. Will he send me an appointment calendar?"

Either because her nerves were on end or because it sounded so ridiculous, Louise went off in a peal of laughter.

Her mother frowned. "I can't imagine what you find so amusing, although," she added darkly, "according to what the Earl said, I wouldn't be surprised if that's how they do it in France. But no, Louise! Women have managed these things since time immemorial! He will say something like *I wish to visit you tonight* and you will say *not tonight my dear, I'm afraid it isn't convenient.*"

"It sounds as if you're making an appointment with the housekeeper!" Louise giggled. Then she controlled herself and said, "But in any case, monthlies or not, isn't it very unpleasant for him and very uncomfortable for me?"

"Gentlemen do not appear to think it unpleasant at all. In fact I believe they all like it a great deal. And yes, it is uncomfortable for us at first, and there is even a small amount of blood. But it gets better. Sometimes, believe it or not, it is even quite pleasant."

"How extraordinary!" said Louise all mirth gone. "The girls at school also said there are women who do this for a living, poor things! The sort of women most gentlemen visit, including my future husband, I suppose?"

"Again, I'm amazed that such discussions should have taken place in an educational establishment. But yes, I'm afraid so."

"What a dreadful way to make a living! One should feel sorry for them, rather than calling them names! They must only do such an unpleasant thing because they have no alternative!"

She thought for a moment. "And really, mama, how is one to learn these things if we women do not talk together? Did you not learn anything from your friends?"

Her mother seemed reluctant to answer but then she said, "Yes, I did, of course, though less, er, graphically than you, perhaps. But well-bred women like us are not expected to know very much about it before we marry."

"It seems to me that the whole relationship between ladies and gentlemen is based upon a series of half-truths and downright lies," said Louise, wonderingly. "We are brought up to believe marriage is the acme of all achievement, the goal to which every maiden must aspire, but in fact it lays us open to unpleasantness and even downright pain. And gentlemen are led to believe we women know nothing of their activities with opera dancers and the like, when in fact we are only too well informed. Really, mama, it's all a tissue of mutual deception!"

"If this is the type of argumentation they encouraged at that school," said her mother shaking her head, "I can only say I understand why your dear papa did not believe in the education of women. I am now inclined to think he was right!"

"Oh mama, don't say that! Don't you see it's education alone which gives us any hope for a future, however distant, when women will no longer be so ignorant about matters essential to their happiness?"

Mrs. Grey looked at her daughter as if she were a changeling. "I can't imagine what your papa would say if he were to hear you," she said. "Or the Earl of Shrewsbury, come to that."

There was a tap at the door and Rose, Louise's maid, came in. She was a very comely girl of sixteen, with a creamy complexion, blue eyes, and blond curls. Having been pretty all her life without needing to make any effort, she knew nothing about helping her mistress to improve her appearance.

She was not above average intelligence, and though she had been lucky enough to go to the village school run by the vicar's wife, she had emerged at the end not much better informed than at the beginning. As is often the case with very good-looking people, their deficits in achievement are more than compensated for by their appearance. It is a rare teacher who will take a lovely girl severely to task for not completing her assignments, and there are always others who will willingly complete them for her.

Rose could read so long as the text were not too difficult, write well enough in a rounded, childish hand and do her sums sufficiently well not to be cheated when she bought her ribbons. Luckily, her duties were limited to seeing to her mistress's linen, keeping her few gowns brushed and ironed, helping her to do them up, and brushing out her braid.

Under normal circumstances she would never have been engaged as a lady's maid, for which she had neither training nor talent. But she was niece to Mrs. Grey's own rather superior dresser Wilkins, and that lady had been pleased to help her sister by arranging her to have the position when Louise came home from school.

In fact, she suited Louise very well, since she was a pleasant, cheerful girl, with a sunny temperament. Being, frankly, rather empty-headed, it never occurred to her to advance an opinion concerning clothing, or anything else. She simply did what she was told.

"Oh, beg pardon, Madam, I didn't know you was here!" she said. "I thought Miss might be wanting to get ready for bed."

"It is getting rather late," said Mrs. Grey, "so you may as well come in."

She turned to her daughter. "I hope you sleep well, my dear. After seeing him again today, I am convinced the Earl will be an admirable husband."

She kissed her daughter's cheek and left.

As she slipped off her old brown dress, Louise knocked to the ground the portfolio into which she had slipped the caricature of the Earl of Shrewsbury. The drawing fell out. Rose picked it up and looked at it in wonder.

"Is that what he looks like then, Miss, your intended?" she asked. She was mentally comparing him to the baker's boy who had been lingering to talk to her at the kitchen door for some weeks. Jimmy was much better-looking, she thought. This man looked like a monkey.

Louise took the drawing from her hand. "Not really. That is, yes, but I've made him look...," how could she explain the image to this girl? "Well, I've made him look much worse than he is."

"But why, Miss?"

"It's called a caricature. It's meant to draw attention to the person's worst characteristics."

Seeing incomprehension in Rose's eyes, she said, "It's just for fun, really."

"Oh."

Rose couldn't understand why anyone would want to make a bad picture of the person they were going to marry. Even for fun. But it did not occur to her to ask for more explanation.

Chapter Seven

The betrothal of the Earl of Shrewsbury and Louise Grey was announced in *The Times* a week later. The wedding was to be at the beginning of June. It caused surprise in nearly every household in the *ton*, for though most mamas had different ideas, their daughters thought him very poor husband material and were astonished he'd found anyone to take him. In the home of one Diane Courtland there was angrily voiced dismay. She had been the Earl's *inamorata* for several months and had begun to entertain real hopes of becoming a Countess. She knew none of the girls in their first or even second season would even look at him. Besides his off-putting appearance, he had a reputation for being cold and distant. That a man as proud as the Earl would not marry a woman with a past did not occur to her. She was confident of her charms.

Gareth visited his betrothed again, to bring her the engagement ring he had removed from the bank vault in which the family jewels were kept. The ring, featuring a large square-cut emerald surrounded by diamonds, was reputed to be Egyptian. When the Earl gave it to her, Louise received it with warm, but not effusive, thanks. In fact, she was delighted, but she thought a dignified demeanor would appeal to her future husband more than loud exclamations of joy. However, her heart, which had given its accustomed leap when she saw him arrive, lurched in her breast again, for it had not occurred to her she would be the recipient of family jewels. She had not agreed to marry the Earl because she wanted a great position, but because she wanted the man.

His lordship was pleased with her gratified but subdued response to the ring. Here was a girl who would not fill his life with drama. Louise curtseyed and lifted her eyes to his with a smile. He surprised himself by leaning forward and kissing her on the cheek. Then he bowed and said he could not keep Jupiter waiting in the cold.

"Of course not," murmured Louise.

They parted, he thinking he had made a wise choice, and she, placing her hand where his lips had been. From the tall drawing room windows she watched him leave, her burning cheek pressed against the cool pane.

The Grey household was surprised, a few days later, to receive a visit from the Earl's grandmother.

Louise was in her mother's bedchamber discussing her wedding gown. Her parent was in the habit of thinking herself purse-pinched, although from what Louise knew of their affairs, they were quite well provided for. Her mother certainly kept herself modishly dressed though she had long ago given up trying to bring her daughter up to snuff. Louise didn't care what she wore. It wasn't worth spending any money on clothes for her.

Mrs. Grey had her dresser unpack her own wedding dress from twenty years before. It was an enormously elaborate affair, the voluminous skirts meant to be worn over a wicker pannier that held the gown wide at the sides. She sighed over its faded loveliness.

"Just look at the four-inch lace around the sleeves alone," she said. "I daresay you couldn't find that today for under fifty pounds! And there's acres of silk in it. What if we get Wilkins to cut it down for you into more modern lines?"

"If you wish, mama," said Louise. "I have no objection, if you think a refurbished gown is quite the thing for a society wedding.

I'm a nobody, but the Earl is very well known. You have seen how proud he is. He might not like it."

"Then it's a pity you didn't ask him for money for bride's clothes. He's rich enough to buy an abbey and wouldn't even miss a few hundred pounds," said her mother.

"Oh, mama, I could never have done such a thing! Anyway, just think how paltry it would have made us look!"

At that moment there was a discreet knock at the bedroom door and her mother's dresser came in.

"The Dowager Countess of Shrewsbury has come to see you, Madam," she announced breathlessly. "Brewster has shown her into the drawing room."

When Louise's betrothal had become known to them, she and the other members of staff had looked the Earl up in Debrett's and they were all well informed of the other members of the family.

"She is the Earl's grandmother, you know," she said now.

Mother and daughter looked at each other in shock. Louise was the first to collect herself. "I'll go down, mama. Take your time."

"But you are looking so dowdy!"

"Am I? Anyway, it doesn't matter. I'm sure the Earl has described me. She won't be surprised. But you will want to look your best."

Her mother was already patting her coiffure into place and wondering if she should change her gown when Louise slipped from the room and ran lightly down the stairs.

Chapter Eight

Louise entered the drawing room to see a well-preserved, slim older lady sitting bolt upright next to the fire. Her ladyship had been taught in her youth not to slouch, and never did so, even when alone.

Lady Esmé Wandsworth, Dowager Countess of Shrewsbury, was beautifully dressed in a fine wool lavender pelisse over what was evidently a matching gown. Her frivolous lacy cap was partially covered by a tan poke bonnet with lavender ribbons that only the strictest of critics would have described as too young for a woman of her age. Next to her neat tan leather boots she held a glass cane with a silver top, and as she began to stand, it was obvious she needed it. Nevertheless, no one would have guessed her age, which Debrett's unflinchingly revealed as 70.

If she'd ever thought about the Earl's grandmother, Louise would have assumed her to be a hook-nosed dowager with a haughty manner like her grandson's. But this lady was nothing of the sort. She made such a pretty picture Louise was entranced. She smiled and came forward with her hand held out. "My lady!" she said, as the older woman began to rise, "Please remain seated! How kind of you to come!"

The Earl's grandmother thus first beheld her future granddaughter-in-law coming towards her, her eyes alight and a smile of welcome on her face. She was certainly plain, and Gareth had been right about her thinness and lack of inches, her dowdy gown and unfashionable coiffure, but there was something in her expression the Dowager liked. She clasped her hand warmly.

"I wanted to be the first to welcome you into the family, my dear," said her ladyship. "Gareth has told me all about you."

Hearing her intended's name used so casually took Louise off guard. She had never yet thought of him as anything but *his lordship*. But her ready humor came to the surface. "It can't have been very much, Ma'am," she said, "we haven't spoken a great deal."

"From what I understand he didn't stay long enough for that! So like a man!" Lady Esmé smiled.

"No. He didn't want to keep his horses waiting in the cold. I quite understood."

"Then you are more generous than I, my dear, I couldn't understand it at all. But no matter. Men are strange creatures, as we know."

At that moment Mrs. Grey came into the room. She had not changed her gown, but she had carefully placed a fine Norwich shawl around her shoulders. The pink silk enhanced the dark hair and vivid complexion which had been her chief claims to beauty in her youth. Now, it must be said, they owed not a little to Wilkins' expert hand. Nonetheless, she presented a much prettier picture than her daughter.

The Earl's grandmother instantly understood. If Mrs. Grey's daughter had been good-looking, she would have been brought up to know it. This had not been the case, and Louise had no doubt grown up in the knowledge she had no claim to beauty. As a result, she made no effort. But from what the Countess could see of it, beneath that ill-fitting gown she was not altogether shapeless, and she definitely had *something*.

She came to a decision. "I was just about to tell Louise, if I may call you that," she said, smiling in her direction, "it is the tradition in the family that the grandmother pay for the wedding dress of her grandson's future wife. Oh dear, that is rather convoluted, but I hope I make myself clear!"

Having invented an altogether fictitious tradition, she lost no time in embellishing it. "My husband's grandmother paid for mine. Oh, I thought myself completely up to snuff! But when I look back on it now, with those wide skirts and reams of lace, I think I must have looked like nothing so much as a galleon in full sail! I'm sure you understand, my dear Mrs. Grey! You are younger than I, to be sure, but the fashions were not so very different when you were wed. That Bonaparte is a scoundrel but one thing that must be said in his favor is that he rid us of those ells of taffeta and the awful cages under our skirts! I'm sure you agree!"

Immediately dismissing the idea of a wedding gown furbished up from her old one, Mrs. Grey nodded her head enthusiastically.

"I propose that Louise come to London next week and stay for a few days. I shall take her to my modiste. Véronique is a positive genius. One may safely leave it to her to fashion a suitable wedding gown. You need not bestir yourself, Mrs. Grey," she added quickly, as she saw her hostess beginning to intervene, "I shall send my own carriage for Louise. She will be quite safe with my groom and her maid."

Louise watched in awe as the Countess dismissed her mother with a charm and ease it was wonderful to behold, then turned the conversation to generalities, the matter settled. She drank a cup of tea, complimented Mrs. Grey on the lightness of the sugar wafer she was offered, ate barely a quarter of it, and took her leave.

Chapter Nine

Two weeks later saw Louise and Rose ensconced in the Countess's comfortable carriage. It was lined in pale pink silk, her ladyship being of the firm belief that when exposed to natural light a woman of her age needed all the help she could get. Rose was wearing the dresser's uniform of a plain dark gown cut high to the throat. It gave her something of the look of a girl pretending to be a grown-up, but it actually suited her fair prettiness, and the color of the carriage lining certainly made her glow even more than usual.

It was hard to say, though, whether Louise was improved by the gentle light. Her mother had loaned her a poke bonnet lined in a bright yellow that suited her own vivid complexion, but did nothing at all to enhance her daughter's sallow coloring. With it she wore a light grey pelisse with matching traveling gown that were too large for her, since they too were on loan from her mother, who was of a more opulent build.

In Louise's trunk were her old brown dress and the new blue sprigged muslin, together with a vivid pink silk day dress and a gold evening gown that had also been her mother's. They had been altered, not altogether successfully, to fit Louise's slimmer figure, and neither color suited her.

Arriving in London, both young ladies were overawed by the Countess's town home, not so much by the building itself, though it was large and elegantly furnished, as by the number of servants.

There seemed to be footmen everywhere and the butler was so superior that if Rose had been told he was the Prince Regent himself, she would have believed it. Louise recovered more quickly than her maid, and was able to greet her ladyship with genuine warmth before being shown to her bedchamber to change out of her traveling clothes and refresh herself before tea.

After helping her mistress, Rose was taken downstairs by one of the footmen who was inclined to be superior towards this country mouse, pretty though she was. But her good looks, unassuming manner and cheerful disposition soon endeared her to the rest of the staff, especially as she was innocent enough not to realize she was being pumped about the future Countess. She sat with a welcome cup of tea at the long pine table where the staff took their meals and willingly answered their questions.

"So she's just come home from school, then?" enquired the housekeeper, "and not Out yet?"

"Well, with her poor papa dying so sudden as he did, she couldn't very well be out gallivantin', could she?"

"And she's quite the bluestocking, you say? Reads the newspaper every day?"

"I don't know about being a bluestocking. But she do say women ought to know as much as men about what's goin' on."

The staff looked at each other in amused shock.

"I wonder if the Earl knows anything about that?" said the footman Peter, who had brought Rose downstairs. "He's very much the Master of the House, even here."

"I agree with her," said Emmie, the chef's assistant, a pert young woman who had plans to improve herself. "No reason why women shouldn't be as hinformed as men. Our brains is almost the same size. I saw a Hexibition at the Royal Society just last year."

"Go on with you! You'd best stick to your pots and pans if you want an 'usband!"

Peter was trying to improve his speech, but occasionally slipped. He had his eye on Emmie and was secretly pleased that she, like him, wanted to move up in the world.

"If yer talkin' about yerself, Peter Simpkins, stand in line. I'm not takin' the first man wot proposes!"

Peter's interest in her hadn't escaped her, and in truth, she wasn't displeased. She knew he had aspirations to the butler's position. That august individual would be retiring in a couple of years and Peter was imitating his speech and his ways. Besides, like all footmen, who were engaged as much for their appearance as for their ability to do the job, he was tall and good-looking.

Emmie herself was learning all she could from the French chef presently employed by her ladyship. The great houses generally had male chefs, but at Shrewsbury House when his French chef had taken off in a fit about something, as they often did, the Earl had simply kept on going with the woman who'd been the chef's assistant. By all accounts, everyone was well pleased with the female chef, though, of course, she was called by the less elevated title of *cook*. When the time came that the Countess's Henri took off for a household offering a greater range for his talents than that of the widowed lady, Emmie would make it known she was ready to step in. But she wasn't about to let Peter Simpkins know how she felt. Let him cook. A stew is always better for a long simmer.

Rose, meanwhile, completely unaware of the currents of romance and intrigue swirling around her, looked at the huge kitchen. Behind the staff dining table stood an enormous open cupboard displaying row after row of blue and white dishes. At the other end of the kitchen were two long work tables covered in all sizes of pots, pans and bowls. On one side was a contraption she had never seen before, into which the chef was now placing a large dish.

"That's a Rumford stove," said the housekeeper, seeing her looking. "What an improvement on the open hearth! You've no idea! Her ladyship doesn't have much to do with kitchens, of course, but the Earl insisted on her having one. Takes a bit of getting used to, of course, but the work you save, not to mention the fuel!"

A little later, when she was upstairs helping her mistress, Rose confided, "There's a big iron thing in the kitchen for the cookin'. I'd be afraid to go anywhere near it. But it was the Earl wanted it, seemingly. They say he's ever so much Master of the house."

"I don't doubt it," was Louise's only reply.

Chapter Ten

When her ladyship informed her grandson of his betrothed's forthcoming visit, he groaned and said he couldn't come to the first night dinner *en famille.* He had another engagement.

"If you think any engagement is more important than seeing your fiancée on her first evening in Town," she told him tartly, "I do not! I expect you to be here."

"Oh, Gran! Spare me!" he answered. "I really don't see the least need."

He had hoped to be able to carry off his betrothal and wedding with as little change to his normal routine as possible.

He had already had to soothe Diane Courtland's ruffled feathers.

"You might at least have told me," she had complained with a brittle smile with which she attempted to conceal her very real disappointment. "Instead of having me read it in the papers like everyone else."

"I didn't think of telling you," he replied. "It makes no difference to us."

"Doesn't it?"

She looked up at him, her eyebrows slightly raised. She had recently discovered one or two tiny wrinkles and had observed that holding her eyes wide helped to smooth them out.

She was what was described in the clubs as *a prime article*, with a generous bosom, tiny waist, and rounded derrière. Her dark hair and green eyes were set off by a creamy complexion she was doing her best to maintain. She presented herself as the widow of a military man, one of the many who had fallen during the Peninsular Wars. In reality, she was the relict of a Midlands mill owner who had fallen, not in military action, but into the slurry from his own mill, while walking home in his cups one night. He had left her well provided for and she had removed to fashionable London with a view to completing her fortunes by, as her mother would have put it, marrying up.

But she liked the intimate company of energetic young gentlemen and had made the mistake of succumbing early on to the temptations of the flesh with a nobleman only just out of his teens. She thought she could keep her indiscretion a secret and marry him. She could do neither. When the young man announced to his startled family that he intended to marry her, they had immediately shipped him off to run their estates in the north and, after some negotiation, agreed to pay her a handsome sum in compensation.

After that there had been several more men, culminating in the Earl of Shrewsbury. She really felt she had hopes there. He was by no means good-looking and his manners were far from conciliating, so it was no surprise he hadn't been able to fix the affections of a young bride. But Diane was sure she could manage him. He was certainly rich enough to make the effort worthwhile. Now she saw his betrothal as a betrayal and knew it would change things between them, no matter what his lordship might say.

"Can you really think it makes no difference to us?" she said now.

"None whatsoever," he answered, pulling her into his arms. She submitted, partly because she enjoyed his embraces, but also thinking, again in her mother's words, that half a loaf was better than none. Until a fresher one came along.

In spite of the Earl's reluctance to dine with his betrothed in intimate company, such was his grandmother's authority that when Louise came down to the drawing room an hour before dinner, the Countess was able to announce, "Gareth will be dining with us. I didn't mention it earlier because he wasn't sure he was able to come, but I have just received a note in confirmation. I'm glad. I hope you two will at last be able to have a conversation of more than a few minutes. No one else will be joining us."

Louise's heart missed a beat. She had expected she would be seeing her betrothed at some point, but hardly thought it would be so soon. Her ladyship had said she need not change for dinner that first night; they were dining *en famille*. She was pleased she was wearing the blue sprigged muslin day dress she had changed into after removing her traveling outfit. She knew she looked better in that than her old brown dress, which was all he had ever seen her in. But then she chided herself. *What difference does it make? He knows what I look like. We are neither of us marrying for looks.*

In fact, when the Earl came into the room nearly an hour later he did notice she looked slightly better. As her mother had said, the muslin gown with its blue sprigs did bring out the color in her wide eyes, but the dressmaker had followed Louise's own instructions not to make it too close fitting or too low in the neck, so the gown was bunchy and did little to reveal her figure beneath. Her hair was still confined in its accustomed tight braid.

"Miss Grey!" The Earl came forward and took her hand, touching his lips to the tips of her fingers. She dipped into a perfectly judged curtsey, murmuring, "My lord."

"Good gracious," cried the Countess, receiving her grandson's kiss on the cheek, "Is it still *Miss Grey* and *my lord*? Where are we? At the Court of St. James?"

Louise was just wondering whether she would ever be able to call her haughty betrothed *Gareth*, when she was saved from responding by the sonorous voice of the butler declaring, "Dinner is served, my lady."

Chapter Eleven

They processed into the dining room, the Earl taking his grandmother on his arm, and the butler leading Louise. The leaves had been removed from the table so that they sat fairly close, the Countess at the head, with Louise and Gareth facing each other.

Her ladyship first discoursed lightly on the latest *on-dits* about town. She did not go into society a great deal these days, her rheumatism paining her if she overdid it, but through a network of friends and acquaintances, kept well abreast of Happenings. The Earl contributed little. As someone who rarely interested himself in gossip, he was not the best informant. He could confirm that Lady Southcott had given birth to twins after five years of a childless marriage. Her husband had been seen, proud as punch, in the clubs.

"Well, the *on-dit* is that he isn't the father," said her ladyship, "but he will be too glad to at last have an heir to question it. Twins! My lady outdid herself! An heir and one for luck!" Then she smiled and said, "But, my dear Louise, this is hardly of interest to you. To have to listen to talk about people one doesn't know is such a bore! Who or what interests you?"

"Well," answered Louise after a pause, "I don't know her, of course, but I wonder if you've heard anything more about the poor former Empress Josephine? I read earlier in the week that her pneumonia was no better. Worse, in fact. Do you know how she goes on? I feel so sorry for her. I know Bonaparte was not our friend, and we're all glad to see him shipped off to Elba, but even though they are no longer married, I believe she still cares for him. It's sad for her to be ill and alone, don't you think?" She looked at them both somewhat apologetically.

The Earl looked at her, his eyebrows drawn together. He seemed rather displeased. "From where do you know about the Empress?"

Louise refused to be daunted. "From the newspaper," she said. "We still get it every day, you see. My mother wanted to cancel it after Papa died, but I begged her to keep it on. I do like knowing what is happening in the world."

"She died today," said the Earl, shortly "She was not alone, however, her son Eugène was with her."

There was a silence while Louise contemplated the sad end of the former Empress of France. The Earl digested the information that his betrothed read the newspaper, and his grandmother smiled inwardly, remembering how not so long ago he had complained about how ill-informed girls were.

"She was only fifty, I believe," said Louise, sadly. Then she sat up and carried on firmly, "And her name will forever be associated with his. It does seem unfair that when husbands are despised for one reason or another, their wives are tarred with the same brush, even if, like the Empress and her husband, they are no longer together."

"But could she not distance herself from him?"

"It seems not. Apparently she loved him, even after their divorce. Anyway, I doubt people would have listened to what she had to say. Women's pronouncements are often put down to ignorance or jealousy. We are rarely credited with any sense."

"Surely that cannot be true!" cried the Countess.

"Oh dear," said Louise, "Forgive me. I didn't mean to run on so. My mama was chastising me only recently for expressing advanced views. She was not at all pleased when she found we girls at school had procured a copy of Mary Wollstonecraft's *Vindication of the Rights of Women*." She was unable to stop herself from continuing, "But even Miss Wollstonecraft doesn't seem to think equality with men is attainable. The best we can hope for is a sort of unequal partnership where the husband at least listens to the views of his wife. But I'm convinced the man's view will almost always prevail."

"Surely you admit a husband's right to be master in his own home?" The Earl looked at her, a frown on his harsh countenance.

Louise saw his look and realized she had gone too far. But she wasn't ready to concede the point.

"I realize there is much to be said on either side and now isn't the moment for such a discussion," she said. "I'm sorry. I don't know how we got onto this topic. It's just that Josephine's situation seemed so sad."

"Your sympathy for another individual surely needs no forgiveness," said the Countess. "And you have every right to express an opinion. The poor woman's situation is not something I have ever considered. I found our discussion most interesting, and I'm sure Gareth did too."

She looked at her grandson and, not for the first time, wished he didn't frown so dreadfully. He looked as if he were really angry, when in fact he was probably just thinking it over. If only he were a little more conciliating. After all, he had been complaining about young women having no opinions to express. Here was one with something to say. His breakfast table might occasionally be a little uncomfortable, but at least it wouldn't be dull.

He inclined his head, but said nothing. No more was said on the topic, but when dinner ended his lordship said he would not stay for port. He had another engagement and hoped they would forgive his too prompt departure.

When they were once more alone, Louise felt she should apologize again for speaking as she had.

"I'm sorry to have cast a pall over the evening," she said. "I think I chased his lordship," she simply couldn't say *Gareth*, "away."

"Nonsense," said the Countess briskly. "It does him good. He is altogether too accustomed to having his own way. You know, my dear, you shouldn't take too much notice of his frowns. He has an unfortunate trick of drawing his eyebrows together over the slightest thing, especially if it's new to him. He often means nothing by it.

"Now, my dear," she continued, "tomorrow morning we are to see the modiste. In the afternoon we shall look in at St. George's Church to confirm the musical selections for your wedding. We also need to show you your future home, of course. But these are all duties, as pleasurable as I hope they will be. Is there anything you would like to do while you are here?"

"I should very much like to go to the British Museum in Montagu House. I understand there is a large collection of antiquities from Egypt. Do you think his lordship could get a ticket for me? I understand one must make an appointment."

The Countess had been thinking more of the hat shops in Cavendish Square, but said immediately, "What a pity we didn't ask him while he was still here. No matter, I'll send him a note. I'm sure he can arrange it."

Chapter Twelve

While this discussion was taking place, the Earl was directing his steps towards Diane Courtland's pretty little house on the edges of Mayfair. He had canceled an invitation to an opening night at the opera with that lady in order to comply with his grandmother's order to be at dinner that evening, and he was sure she would not be happy.

The conversation with his betrothed had unsettled him. What did the chit think she was about, with her talk of the rights of women? He had been willing to offer for a plain, quiet woman. And now this! He conveniently forgot that it was the hint of a challenge that had drawn him to this particular plain, quiet woman in the first place.

When he arrived, he found he was right. Diane was full of her disappointment at not going to the opera.

"Gareth, my dear," she pouted, "I'm surprised to see you here. I thought you were busy all evening. I'm so disappointed, I can't tell you. I'm sure all the *ton* was there. It's most vexing!"

"I told you I was sorry, but my grandmother wouldn't take no for an answer. If you want to know the truth, my betrothed wife is staying with her for a few days. I would have avoided it if I could."

"La! Is she such an antidote then? You looked like thunder when you came in!"

The Earl was conscious of having made a mistake both in mentioning Louise and letting his feelings show. Now he was angry with himself for discussing his wife-to-be with his mistress. If he hadn't been so preoccupied with Louise's assertions, he would never have done so.

"Certainly not." His tone admitted no further discussion.

"Well, she obviously isn't charming enough to make you stay." Diane came to him and wound her plump white arms around his neck.

"Hmm." He kissed her. "Let's not talk about it anymore. There are more pleasant ways to pass the time."

"I don't see why I should want to pass any time with you after you let me down so disgracefully. You are going to have to make it up to me somehow."

Gareth sighed. He could see where this was leading.

"What do you want?" he said baldly.

"We...ell, since you ask, you remember the lovely emerald pendant you gave me last month?"

"Yes."

"Well, Garrard's have earrings in their window that would match it perfectly."

"I'll have them sent over tomorrow."

Diane was delighted. Emerald earrings were better than an evening at the opera. One could not put an opera in one's jewel box against a rainy day. For she had no faith at all in the Earl's protestations that his marriage would make no difference to their relationship.

So much would depend on his wife. Diane wished she knew what she looked like. Obviously she didn't have the face or the skill to keep him by her side. Or it could be that she didn't care to. Perhaps she was the sort to ignore her husband while pursuing conquests of her own. There were *haut ton* couples, she knew, who barely ever saw each other. She was one of the people who believed Lady Southcott's twins had a father other than her husband. As far as she knew, the Southcott couple didn't even live in the same house. But the Earl of Shrewsbury was a proud man and she doubted he would ever contemplate an open marriage. And she knew him well enough to know that neither would he tolerate scenes.

Diane had already begun to cast her eye around for her next protector. She had fluttered her very long eyelashes at the dashing Denis Youngbrough, newly arrived in town and evidently with money to spend. She wanted to have someone in the wings in case of necessity. She had always preferred younger men. Her skills beguiled them more than they did their more experienced fraternity. But it wasn't easy.

She remembered the youth she had attracted when she first arrived in London. He had been prepared to be cut off entirely from his family rather than give her up. She smiled ruefully recalling the delicacy with which she had been obliged to extricate herself from his youthful schemes for their penniless future. She had begged him with tears in her eyes not to ruin himself for her, to go to run the family estates as his papa wanted. She told him he would forget her, and since a few years later he had married an altogether unexceptionable young woman from a good family, she had to suppose he had.

Of course, Shrewsbury wasn't easy either. He rarely gave away his feelings and she now saw she'd made a mistake in thinking them deeper than they were. That was a pity because she might be the teensiest bit in love with him. Like Louise, she had not found his ugly face and ape-like figure off-putting, quite the reverse. His power often made her shiver with excitement. Perhaps he was right: a wife wouldn't make any difference. In the meantime, though, she would keep Youngbrough in the wings and play on her justified sense of ill-usage to extract what she could from the Earl. In fact, Diane and Louise had a good deal in common: they were both drawn to Gareth Wandsworth and they both believed in the rights of women. It was just that Diane's ideas of what those rights were, were different.

Chapter Thirteen

Louise came downstairs the next morning prepared for the visit to the modiste. She was wearing her pink day dress, the rather ill-fitting grey pelisse, and the only bonnet she had, with the yellow lining.

Her ladyship regarded her with a critical eye. "Hmm... the cut of that pelisse is surely for a lady larger than you, my dear," she said. "Let me see. You and I are of a size, I believe. Ring the bell for me, please."

When the butler arrived with his stately tread, the Countess said, "Have Booth meet me and Miss Grey in my rooms."

Booth was the Countess's long-time dresser. When Louise and the Countess arrived, their progress being necessarily slow, she was already there. She looked Louise up and down and raised her eyebrows slightly.

"Exactly!" said her ladyship. "Something has to be done. The pelisse is too large and the pink of the gown and the yellow of the bonnet lining are an unfortunate combination. I think that navy pelisse of mine, don't you? I don't think I've worn it above twice. We'll make sure it's buttoned all the way up to cover as much of the pink as possible. And we must have some matching ribbon to trim the bonnet somewhere!"

The dresser was gone for several minutes but returned with the navy pelisse over her arm and a bunch of ribbon in her hand. She helped Louise out of the over-large grey garment and into the blue one.

"Much better!" declared the Countess. "Now, Booth, dear, do something with the bonnet. The shape suits Miss Grey well enough, but that lining doesn't become her at all."

The dresser took the bonnet gently from Louise's head. She sat in a low chair for a few minutes, twisting and wrapping, ending with the ribbon braided around the crown of the bonnet, tied in rosettes on the sides and ending loose for tying under the chin. The navy blue ribbons went a long way to moderating the effect of the yellow-lined poke.

"How clever!" cried Louise, "and so pretty! Thank you both so very much!"

"Yes. I don't know what I should do without my Booth," said her ladyship, smiling at that lady. "Do you have a dresser, my dear?"

"Yes, though she's more just a maid, really. But she… well, she suits me."

"I see," said her ladyship, doubtfully. It was clear that whoever she was, the bride-to-be's girl didn't know her business.

The girl in question was at that moment blushing at the bold attentions of the young man who delivered the newspaper to her ladyship's establishment. The Countess rarely looked at it, but it was still ironed smooth and placed in the library every morning. Normally it sat there most of the day until the butler took it to his sitting room. He enjoyed reading it with the glass (or two) of port he allowed himself from his employer's cellars.

Freddy, the newspaper delivery boy, was a bright, cheeky, and good-looking young man born and bred in the City of London. The world of newspapers fascinated him. Nowadays the printing machines featured cylinders that pressed the words onto both sides of the paper as if by magic. They were run by steam engines and he loved the hot, smoky, incredibly noisy room where they were located. To some it might have seemed like a devil's playground, but to him it had the sound and smell of money.

One day he had ventured upstairs to where a row of reporters sat at desks, calling to each other, making facetious remarks and sometimes writing. He fell into conversation with one of them and discovered that their job was to find out what was going on and write about it, not only in London and the rest of Great Britain, but in the whole world. His new friend's specialty was writing what was essentially gossip about those he called The Nobs, or the upper classes.

"Everyone likes to read about them," he said. "If you haven't got money they fascinate you, and if you have, you want to see what they're up to so's you can do the same, or see how much better off you are."

Freddy couldn't write much more than his name, and he'd never been further afield than the Mile End Road, but he was good at finding out things. His good looks belied the fact he was nosy and unscrupulous.

Women liked Freddy. The older ones were inclined to mother him and the younger ones responded to his handsome face and the twinkle in his eye. He found that by engaging the female staff at the kitchen doors where he delivered his papers, he learned a lot. It was he who'd given his friend the story about Lady Southcott's twins. His friend on the newspaper had paid him ten shillings for that one. He was proud to tell Rose he had sold a story, but luckily she didn't ask what sort, and he didn't say.

He was pumping her for whatever she could tell him. It wasn't a great deal more than everyone already knew. The Earl of Shrewsbury was marrying a nobody.

"What's she like then, his *feeongsay*?"

"Oh, she's ever so nice. Never a cross word from her lips."

"No lovers in the past, no baby born on the other side of the blanket, or anything like that?"

Rose was scandalized. "No, of course, not. She's a lady!"

"That's what they all say!" He patted her cheek. "An innocent girl like you, you don't know the 'alf of it! Anyway, when's yer day off?"

"I'm only here another two days."

"No!" Freddy was disappointed. This naïve country girl could be a good source of information.

"When yer comin' back?"

"At the end of the month for the wedding, and then we'll be moving to Shrewsbury House, seemingly."

"Where's that, then?"

"I don't know. I don't know where anything is in London."

"Well, Rose, I'll find it and when yer gets back I'll take yer on a tour. How 'bout that?"

"That'd be lovely!"

She firmly pushed Jimmy back home out of her mind. She was going to live in London, wasn't she? She didn't want a bumpkin like him anyway.

Chapter Fourteen

Her ladyship's dressmaker Véronique was set up in an exclusive establishment not far, in fact, from Diane Courtland's little house. She had come to London from Paris twenty-five years before, the dressmaking *atelier* in which she had been working since the age of fourteen having been burned to the ground. The men who had done the burning did so because they disapproved of the members of the aristocracy who had their elaborate gowns made there. Not one of those elegant ladies had been in the shop at the time. The only one to perish was Véronique's employer, a skillful, hardworking woman who, after her husband died of the fever, had struggled all her life to keep a roof over her and her children's heads.

Véronique had seen the writing on the wall and had left Paris immediately. She had made her way to London and begun again, doing menial tasks in a fashionable modiste's until her very real talents had been discovered. She had risen quickly, ultimately becoming chief designer and then co-owner of the establishment. When her partner died, she had re-named the shop and concentrated on catering to only the very wealthy. The Countess had been her customer for years.

Nowadays, she herself took on very few clients. She was a lady of advancing years, looking forward to a well-earned retirement. She still oversaw everything that went out of the shop and had an eagle eye for the slightest error in fit or style. But her assistants did all the work.

When she saw Louise, however, she immediately took care of her personally. This was because she recognized in her someone like herself. She had spent her years working amongst beautiful women, but had never been one of them. She was downright plain, with a flat face, receding chin, wide nose and thin, wispy hair. However, she dressed with such quiet elegance that anyone who knew her would have been surprised to hear her called that.

When the Countess explained that Louise was wanting a wedding gown, she looked the bride-to-be up and down and said, half to herself, "Yes. I see. Mademoiselle is not in the ordinary way." "You will forgive me," she said, addressing herself to Louise, "You have not beauty in the face and it could be wished you were a little more tall. But you have a good carriage and though you are too thin, from what one may observe beneath your garment — I do not call it a gown — you have a shape. Yes, we must make sure the eye is drawn to that. Fit will be all. This I understand for myself, as you see. The... *objet* you are wearing is not for you. The color is *affreuse* and it has been altered, but badly. No," she said again, "it is not for you. No. *Certainement non*."

Louise thought it a good thing her mother was not there to hear this unvarnished assessment, but before she was able to utter a word, she was ushered into a curtained alcove, where the offending garment was ruthlessly removed. She was then subjected to being pushed this way and that, being measured from all possible angles.

That having been accomplished, she was given a silk wrapper and brought into Véronique's *atelier*. It was rare indeed these days for a customer to be invited to this inner sanctum and the word soon went round. *The Earl of Shrewsbury's betrothed* was on the lips of everyone in the establishment, from the girl who swept the floor to the head cutter, who worked for no one but Véronique's top clients.

It happened that Diane Courtland was there. Since she had been under the generous protection of the Earl she had been able to have several gowns made in that exclusive establishment, though not by Véronique herself. The words came to her ears also, and she contrived to catch a glimpse of the bride-to-be as she was bustled from one place to the other.

"Why, she's nothing but a plain little country mouse," she said to herself with satisfaction. "I don't need to worry after all. She won't keep Gareth's attention for more than a week."

Having completed her business she left, feeling pleased with herself.

Unaware that she had been seen and recognized, over the next hour Louise gave herself entirely into Véronique's hands. She and the Dowager Countess sat with the modiste looking at models in the *Mode Parisienne,* most of which Véronique dismissed with an impatient hand. "*Non et non,*" she declared. "Mademoiselle will not wear lace, frills, flounces, wide sleeves, or a mass of ribbons! We do not seek to hide, we seek to show what is fine!"

Then came bolts of silk.

"*Non et non!*" she cried again when an assistant produced a roll of pure white silk. "Look at the complexion of Mademoiselle! She cannot wear this white. Find me an ivory!"

Silks were piled up on the large table sitting in the center of the atelier. For the first time in her life, Louise began to understand how much color mattered. And fit mattered. She had never paid much attention to how her gowns hung upon her body, except to not want them too low cut or narrow, which she believed accentuated her thinness.

Véronique pointed out that not only did the bright pink dress she was wearing make her color even more sallow, it was too wide and bunched beneath her bosom, making her look round and shapeless. To be sure, the Empire style gowns did not fit into the waist, but they should not give the impression that Mademoiselle had no waist at all! A trim midsection gave value to the bosom. And the neckline was cut too high, *voyons!* Miss Grey must see that it made her neck appear even shorter. She must wear gowns with the bodice cut into a vee. This would elongate the neck. It was evident!

They finally settled upon a wedding gown of simple lines, falling from beneath the bosom, narrow in front, with long fitted sleeves and a vee neckline cut low enough to just hint at the fullness beneath. It would button with a row of pearls from the nape of the neck to the center of the back, from where the silk would fall in pleats to a train. This could be caught up on the wrist after the ceremony. The simplicity was deceptive, said the modiste, sketching all the time she spoke. Everything would be in the fit!

The headdress gave them the most trouble, for Véronique persuaded them nothing should ruin the elegant back view of the gown. It was, after all, what most people saw for the greatest length of time. A long veil would ruin the line, and an abbreviated one would make Mademoiselle look as if she had no neck. It was the Dowager Countess who hit on the solution. Louise would wear no veil at all. Her abundant hair would be dressed on the top of her head, with a few natural ringlets over her ears, and she would wear a tiara. Her ladyship had just the thing at home.

The bride-to-be was then helped back into her pink gown, noting all the things she now knew were wrong with it. After a cup of tea, she and her future grandmother-in-law left Véronique, who promised to send the gown to the London house in good time for the ceremony at the end of the month. The Dowager Countess had invited both Louise and her mother there to stay before the wedding.

Before they left, Louise spoke privately with the modiste for a few minutes.

"I shall be needing a complete wardrobe once I am married. May I count on you?"

"Of course, Mademoiselle. *Moi*, I know *exactement* what you need. You have just to send me a note and it shall be done!"

With thanks and salutations on both sides, they parted in mutual appreciation, each with her own plans. For Véronique it was the determination that the dressing of the new Countess of Shrewsbury would be her last and finest achievement. For Louise, it was to think how best to use what she had learned.

When the Dowager Countess realized Louise had never even seen the place in which she was to be married, she had arranged for them to visit St. George's Church on the way home from the modiste's. There wasn't a great deal to discuss, since, as she said, all weddings were much the same, apart from the bride's gown. So it proved to be. The organist proposed two pieces by Handel, who had himself been a frequent worshipper at the church about a hundred years before. Louise wasn't familiar with either of them, but the Dowager nodded her head. The service itself would, of course, be the one prescribed in the Book of Common Prayer. Louise had nothing to add, and she could tell the Dowager was flagging; the consultation at Véronique's had been long and tiring. So she willingly agreed to everything they said, and they were soon back in the carriage.

They dined quietly and went early to bed. The visits to Shrewsbury House and the Museum were the next day. Louise was anxious about both. She wanted to see where she would be living but was afraid it might be terribly grand. Luckily, the Dowager was coming with her and she could take her cues from her. It was her former home, of course. But she was to go alone with Gareth to the Museum. She was simultaneously elated and anxious at the prospect of spending those hours alone with her fiancé. Sleep did not come quickly.

Chapter Fifteen

"I hope it will not tire you too much coming with me to Shrewsbury House, my lady," said Louise the following morning. "Yesterday was very fatiguing for you."

"Nonsense!" replied the Dowager. "I'm looking forward to seeing the old place. Besides, I need to make sure they've been keeping it up to snuff. Remember, my dear, lazy employers make lazy servants. And Gareth just assumes everything will be done as it should be. Luckily, the housekeeper Mrs. Smith is a good woman and the butler Lisle has been with him forever."

Thus, after a leisurely breakfast the Dowager Countess ordered the carriage and the two women sallied forth to Louise's future home.

"I found Shrewsbury House altogether too large for me alone after my husband died," said the Countess as they mounted the broad white stone steps to the front door. They were flanked by a pair of fine plane trees that shaded the front of the house. "And Gareth had no objection to moving in, so I was pleased to leave. But it has always been perfect for entertaining. I daresay it has the largest private ballroom in London. In fact, I am sending out invitations for the Ball here to present you to the *ton* a couple of weeks after you are married. Normally, your mama-in-law would do it, but of course...." Her voice broke off.

Louise's heart lurched when she heard about the Ball, but seeing the Dowager's distress, she pressed her hand and said, "I'm so sorry."

Her ladyship lifted her chin and gave her a tremulous smile. "It's a dreadful thing to lose a child. I pray you never have such a misfortune, my dear. But," she said, lifting her chin, "it's no good crying over it now. We must look to the future. I'm glad Gareth is marrying you, Louise. I think you will deal very well together and I want to see a great-grandson before I die."

Then, as the butler opened the wide front door, she said in a quite different tone, "Good morning, Lisle. I am bringing Miss Grey to see over the house. Is the Earl in?"

"Good morning, my lady," he answered with a bow, "No, his lordship is at the House this morning. He begs you to excuse him and says he will return for luncheon and to escort Miss Grey to the Museum this afternoon. Mrs. Smith is expecting you."

Louise didn't know whether to be glad or sorry her betrothed wasn't there. She digested the information that he was at the House of Lords. She hadn't realized he took his responsibilities there seriously.

Meanwhile, the housekeeper was making a deep curtsey to her former mistress and her future one, taking in the latter with a quick, shrewd glance.

"I've taken the holland covers off and opened the curtains in the drawing and dining rooms, my lady," she said, not finding it necessary to reveal that the staff had all been hard at work for days to clean and polish every inch of the house. "They've been unused this age because his lordship never goes in there. He generally sits in the library and uses the breakfast room when he dines alone at home. Of course, we will be using the dining room for the wedding breakfast."

This was the first Louise had heard of this event, too, but the Dowager merely nodded as if it were a foregone conclusion. They trooped into the large, elegant rooms, clearly designed for entertaining on a grand scale.

"I'm glad to see those curtains haven't faded too much," said the Dowager, indicating the long drapes in the tall window embrasures.

"Yes, my lady," replied the housekeeper. "We keep them closed to protect the carpet and paintings, but we're lucky the trees in front protect them from the afternoon sun."

"My predecessor grew up on a huge estate in the country," remarked the Dowager, "and wanted to have trees and gardens around her to remind her of her family home. Her instincts in that respect were excellent, though her taste in furnishings was, unfortunately, less good. When I think of all that dark William and Mary stuff — it was so gloomy! I had to change everything."

Louise looked at the graceful, slim-legged Hepplewhite furniture with its light-colored silk upholstery, and thought how little the beautiful room reflected the man who lived there. "This is lovely," she said. "I should hate to change anything."

"Thank you, my dear," replied the Dowager, patting her hand, "but the new Countess must have full freedom to make her home how she wants it. My dear son's wife would probably have done so had they ever lived here."

When they were about to go upstairs, Louise said, "I should like to see the library, if I may."

The housekeeper inclined her head and led them across the hall. As soon as the door was opened, a masculine scent of cigars, leather and old books met Louise's nose. She looked around. The walls were lined with crowded bookshelves enclosed in glass cabinets. It was obvious they were not there merely for show, and the general effect was one of comfort, not display. Yes, she could see the Earl in here, his broad shoulders in the wide leather chairs next to the big fireplace, the newspaper in his lap and a glass of something on one of the sturdy dark wood tables next to him. Evidently, this room had not been subjected to his grandmother's refurbishment; everything looked as if it had been there forever.

As if reading her mind, the Dowager Countess said, "As you can see, my husband refused to have anything changed in here, and Gareth prefers it to any other room."

Louise smiled and nodded, then they all turned back to the staircase which rose gracefully from the center of the hall.

Once upstairs, Louise's heart beat faster as the housekeeper opened a door to a room saying, "These will be your apartments, Miss Grey," then turning to the Countess, added, "They remain how they were when you were in residence, your ladyship."

They stepped into a lovely sitting room. Light flooded in from the high windows hung with flimsy curtains beneath silk drapes in her ladyship's characteristic rose. A delicate settee and bergère chairs were grouped for conversation on top of a pretty Aubusson rug. Small tables were dotted around the room, bearing vases of flowers and a few decorative objects. Nothing could have been a more striking contrast to the dark furniture and the deep reds and blues of the Turkish rug in the library.

"It looks a bit bare in here," said her ladyship. "I took my personal collection of Sèvres with me. But you will be able to fill it with items of your own taste."

Louise thought of her caricatures and smiled inwardly. That was definitely not what her future grandmother-in-law intended.

"It's lovely as it is," she said. "I don't think I could do anything to improve it."

This remark pleased both her ladyship and the housekeeper, the first because it seemed to confirm the new Countess would be led by her in matter of taste, and the second because she considered a becoming docility appropriate in a new bride.

They passed into the bedchamber which was furnished in the same style as the sitting room. The big high bed had pale pink hangings, tied back with corded tassels. The pretty matching coverlet was edged with ivory lace and embroidered all over in openwork flowers. It was enchantingly feminine and as unlike Louise's bedroom at home as could be imagined. There, she still slept in the narrow bed of her youth and the covers and hangings were of simple linen.

"His lordship's rooms are next door," said Mrs. Smith as they traversed the sitting room once more. She indicated a door that communicated between the two apartments. Louise would have loved to open the door, but it wasn't proposed and she dared not ask.

The tour was evidently at an end, for the housekeeper announced, "The ballroom is on this floor, but it hasn't been used since his lordship has been in residence. We haven't taken off the covers yet, so unless you object, I won't take you in there, Miss Grey. Besides, the Earl will be here soon for luncheon and you know he dislikes tardiness. He instructed it to be laid out in the breakfast room, so if you would come this way...."

They were led back downstairs and into a pleasant room with French windows. These stood half open and gave onto a pretty garden at the back of the house. A pathway led to a fountain that sparkled in the sun. Beyond it was an arbor now covered in early roses. Inside the room, one of the walls was decorated with a *trompe l'oeil* painting of the same view. It showed the French windows wide open, the path to the fountain and the floral arbor, and younger versions of the trees that now stood at full height. The effect was charming.

"I think it one of the prettiest private gardens in London," said the Dowager. "As I said, my predecessor was responsible for it. She was so fond of it she had this wall painted after seeing a similar *trompe l'oeil* on the Continent."

Louise was entranced. "It's wonderful!" she said. "It's like having two gardens!"

The other walls of the room were painted a pale green that blended nicely with the *trompe l'oeil*. On one of them there were portraits of a man and a woman. Louise saw immediately that the man must have been the Earl's father. He had the same lowering brow and large hooked nose. The woman in the other portrait was petite and pretty, though otherwise unremarkable. Her face showed no particular character. *So that was his mother,* she thought. *He seems to have nothing of her in him.*

"My late son and his wife," confirmed the Dowager Countess. "The portraits were done just before they left for China. Gareth asked me to leave them here when I moved. They are all he had left of his parents, poor boy."

For the first time, Louise thought of her future husband as the boy he must have been, learning that his Mama and Papa had perished so far away. When he left them to go to school in England he couldn't have known that he would never see them again. And he wanted to keep these images of them in the room he apparently used every day. Her heart was touched.

Chapter Sixteen

The object of Louise's sympathy arrived a few minutes later. The Earl greeted his grandmother with a kiss on the cheek, but to her he bowed and said formally, "I'm sorry not to have been here to welcome you, Louise. I hope everything has met with your approval."

Her heart had done its usual somersault when he came in and then hearing him use her Christian name for the first time, she hardly knew what she was saying. "No... yes, I mean, everything is perfect. Thank you for inviting me to visit."

He raised his eyebrows. "This is to be your home, after all," he replied, somewhat sardonically.

She blushed and looked down in confusion. "Yes... of course. I...."

But thankfully, he seemed to require no more of an answer, for he said in his normal brusque manner, "I am in the habit of lunching here and thought it better than the dining room for an informal meal. But we'd better sit down. Our appointment at the Museum is for three and I should not like to be late."

He pulled out his grandmother's chair, while the butler did the same for Louise, and they sat.

"Don't waste any time, Lisle," said the Earl. "Bring it in."

The meal was simple: cold meats and fruit, but everything was of the finest, particularly the fruit.

"Have you these strawberries from Overshott, Gareth?" said her ladyship, shaking sugar over the fruit from a pretty slotted spoon, and although they were quite small, cutting them in half before conveying them to her mouth. "I must say, they have been wonderful this year." She turned to Louise. "Our place in the country, you know. Gareth will take you there soon. At the end of the summer there will be grapes from the hothouses. We are quite famous for them. I know some people dislike grapes, because of the seeds. But our fruit is large enough to cut in half and take them out. I remember my mother would never eat a grape unless it was seeded and sometimes peeled for her, but we are more self-sufficient these days. I have no trouble with them at all."

Louise served herself some strawberries and prepared them the same as the Dowager. They were delicious. The Earl sat there absently dipping the berries whole into the sugar and eating them with his fingers. *How nice to be a man* she thought. *I wonder if the day will ever arrive when we women can sit at table eating fruit with our fingers like that?*

Gareth wasn't looking forward to wasting his afternoon at the British Museum. There was a boxing match he wanted to go to. He was a follower of the Fancy, as it was commonly called, and a keen boxer himself. He had the build for it, combined with considerable talent. Gentleman Jackson, who ran the popular boxing saloon on Bond Street, had more than once told him it was a pity he was a toff, because he could have made his fortune in the ring. When his grandmother had proposed the excursion with Louise he had made excuses, but ironically, it was Diane who changed his mind.

"I saw the future Countess at Véronique's," she declared. "La, my lord! One cannot call her a beauty! I wish you very happy, I'm sure!"

"One does not necessarily look for beauty in a wife," he replied. "There are other qualities that are more desirable."

"Like being a bluestocking, I collect," answered she, for in a moment of discontent he had talked about Louise wanting to visit the museum.

He had not denied it, and then felt guilty he had been foolish enough to discuss his future wife with her. In the end it was his sense of guilt that drove him to accompany his future wife.

As it turned out, Louise did not have as much time alone with her future husband that afternoon as she had imagined. They were met at the museum by Joseph Planta, Principal Librarian, who was obviously delighted to give them a comprehensive tour of the old Montagu mansion. The various rooms had been turned into book-lined galleries with cabinets of curiosities down the center. Gareth had not expected to enjoy it, but found himself drawn in, not least by Louise's reactions to what they saw.

Planta was a bibliophile and took them first to the priceless Cotton Collection. This was the work of three generations of the Cotton family and contained the only remaining examples of many early books and legal documents. These had been saved by family members after the dissolution of the monasteries or from careless storage in private libraries. The first Cotton, a Sir Robert, had decided to catalog the items by the name of the bust mounted atop the bookcase they were housed in. Thus, if you wanted the only copy in existence of the Anglo-Saxon Lindisfarne Gospels, catalogued as *Nero D iv*, you would find it in the bookcase with a bust of the Roman Emperor Nero on top, on the fourth shelf (D), book four (iv).

Louise found this amusing. "I wonder what mad old Nero would have thought," she said, "to know that one day a likeness of him would be standing above the Four Gospels. He is well known to have persecuted Christians in his day, but it seems now he stands guard over them!"

They then went to see the famous Elgin Marbles, which were crowded into a space that was really too small for the proper appreciation of them.

"The Greeks obviously didn't have the same view of women as we do now," Louise commented as she stood in front of the more than life-size female figures labelled as being Hestia, Dione, and her daughter Aphrodite. "Their large size must indicate how important they were."

"But they are goddesses," replied the Earl. "They were thought to have enormous power. I imagine it was thought best to propitiate them."

"So you think women should only be propitiated if they have enormous power?"

"You are deliberately misinterpreting my words, Miss Grey," said her fiancé, "but I think I am beginning to recognize your tendency to be provoking."

Louise turned her wide eyes on him. They were dancing. "If you say so, my lord," she said demurely.

For her part, she was beginning to see what the Dowager had said was true. The frown on her betrothed's face was simply how he faced the world. It was because his eyebrows grew together and his brow was so heavy. Most of the time, he wasn't really frowning at all.

"We are sadly overcrowded here now," commented Planta, who had paid no attention to this exchange. "I shouldn't complain, but every British nobleman who acquires anything on his world travels inevitably gives them, or sells them, to us."

Probably because his wife refuses to have them in the house, thought Louise. *Think of the cleaning! And the embarrassment of the maids if they had to dust the statues' private parts!*

But she did not voice this view of the matter, lest she be *provoking*.

The Earl stayed to dine with his grandmother and his wife-to-be, and found himself quite enjoying it. Between Louise's descriptions of what they had seen, and his and his grandmother's recounting of some of the odd objects their friends had in their homes, relics of an ancestor's wanderings, they passed a pleasant evening.

"So what did her *future ladyship* have to say about the museum, then?" enquired Diane, putting ironic emphasis on the words, when Gareth saw her later that night.

"She showed the proper appreciation of the objects there," he answered shortly, annoyed at her tone and the fact that, once again, he was being interrogated about his future wife.

Diane, recognizing his annoyance, said no more.

Chapter Seventeen

Louise and Rose returned home the next day. Louise was quiet in the carriage. In spite of the trip to London, her approaching marriage seemed unreal. She still didn't know the man she was to marry. He said he was beginning to recognize her tendency to be provoking. What was she beginning to recognize in him? She had had an inkling of his softer feelings in his desire to keep his parents' portraits and he certainly treated his grandmother with affection. But he treated her with as much formality as a mere acquaintance. After that one time, he'd never even kissed her cheek.

Rose was quiet too, but in her case it was because she was dwelling on the fine time she had enjoyed. She had loved London. The other staff members had treated her with kindness and even respect. She'd been seated just below the Countess's dresser at the kitchen table. When her lady was married and at her own establishment, only the butler and the housekeeper would be higher than her. And then there was Freddy! He'd promised to show her around. She couldn't wait to get back.

In the weeks before the wedding, Mrs. Grey suggested Louise have some new gowns made in preparation for her entry into London society.

"No," said her daughter. "The Countess says we won't receive any invitations for at least two weeks, so I shan't need them. I'll have time to order a wardrobe from Véronique. Apparently it's the custom to leave newlyweds alone until they make the first move by sending out invitations of their own. Her ladyship is hosting a Ball at Shrewsbury House to present me, as I told you. You're coming, aren't you, Mama? Why don't you order yourself a ballgown instead?"

This idea found so much favor with Mrs. Grey that no more was said about her daughter's lack of wardrobe.

There was little for Louise to do, in fact. She rather inexpertly embroidered her initials on her handkerchiefs and underclothing so they would not get lost in what she was sure was the mountain of laundry at Shrewsbury House, and met with friends in the neighborhood to wish them goodbye. It was not the custom to travel far for a wedding, and they were not expected to make the trip.

She saw nothing of and heard nothing from her future husband. In fact, the next time Louise saw him was when he stood by her side in St. George's Church. She and her mother had arrived back in London the day before and had stayed with the Dowager Countess overnight. Even now, she knew, her trunks were being transported to Shrewsbury House. Tonight she would lie in that pink silk bed. She tried not to think about it, but it had been the only thing on her mind as the wedding day drew closer. Last night she had not slept a wink. Now she was too tired, nervous, and overwrought to take in the details of her surroundings.

Her heart was pounding so loud in her ears as she walked down the aisle, she knew the organ was playing, but had no idea what the music was. She was alone: she had no father to accompany her and her mother was already sitting in the front pew. There were people there, but their faces were a blur. Her whole concentration was on putting one foot in front of the other.

The assembled company saw a young woman advancing down the aisle in an ivory silk gown. Only the most naïve of the onlookers thought it a simple gown, however. The fit was one that could be achieved by only the most superior modiste, and the elegance of the whole ensemble was stunning. She carried a bouquet of lilies exactly the color of her gown and wore no veil. Her hair was wound into a simple arrangement on top of her head and around it a tiara sparkled with diamonds in the mid-morning light.

That morning, the Dowager and her dresser had come in as Louise sat at her dressing table in her stockings and petticoat, her mother watching with exasperation as Rose tried to arrange her curls on the top of her daughter's head.

"It all just keeps falling down!" she wailed.

"You stupid girl!" cried Mrs. Grey, herself handsomely coiffed and dressed in a vivid green that admirably became her dark hair and eyes.

"Give it here," said Booth, taking over.

In minutes, Louise's abundant hair was tamed into submission, held on the top of her head with loose ringlets over her ears. Then the Countess produced a black box, which, when opened, revealed a pretty tiara. It was fashioned like a daisy chain a child might make in the meadows, except that the daisies' petals were oval diamonds with a pearl in the center of each flower.

"I wore this when I was a young bride," she said, "but I'm too old for it now."

Before Louise could say a word, Booth took the crown and fastened it around her curls. Then she, the Dowager Countess and Louise's mother stood back and looked at their handiwork.

"Perfect!" They all said together.

"But... but...," stammered Louise. "I had no idea it would be anything so costly."

"Tush!" said the Countess in a tone that brooked no disagreement. "I am delighted you should wear it at your wedding and I hope I shall live long enough to see your daughter do the same. Now, let Booth help you into your gown so we can all see the full effect."

Booth laid a sheet on the carpet, arranged the wedding gown with all its buttons undone on top, and helped Louise to step into it. Then she pulled it up over her slim hips, helped her into the sleeves, and did up all the pearl buttons down the back. It fit perfectly. In front, the silk fell narrowly to her feet from beneath a bodice that revealed the swell of her breasts. The vee neckline and the elegant coiffure elongated her neck. As she turned to look at herself in the mirror, the other ladies could see that the long row of buttons from the back of the neck to the center of her back where the soft folds of the train began had the same lengthening effect. It was a triumph.

Their breath produced an "Oh!" of wonder. Louise walked forward to the mirror. She saw her own face, but there ended all resemblance to her usual self. An elegant lady stood before her, her hair gracefully swept up and sparkling with the diamonds in the morning light.

It was Rose who said it best.

"Ooh, Miss," she breathed. "You do look a treat! That's the loveliest gown I ever seen!"

Louise picked up the sheaf of lilies Véronique had sent her with the note:

Elegant flowers for an elegant bride.
With the compliments of Véronique Aigner.

She turned, holding the lilies with their long matching ribbon.

"Perfect!" sighed the assembled ladies, again.

In St. George's Chapel, the Earl of Shrewsbury turned and beheld his betrothed walking towards him. At least, it was her same plain face, her wide grey eyes now filled with anxiety, but she seemed somehow taller and more shapely. His dark eyes flickered in appreciation and he bowed.

Then the service began.

Afterwards, Louise wouldn't have been able to repeat what the rector said, what the Earl replied or what her words had been. She knew he had placed a ring on her finger, for there it was, and she knew she had signed a huge register where a finger had pointed. But suddenly, they were walking back up the aisle, man and wife, and the organ was playing something that sounded like trumpets.

Outside, she was dazzled by the brilliant summer sunshine. She was aware of people waving and shouting. The Earl took her elbow firmly and led her to a waiting carriage. He helped her in, then turned and, drawing handfuls of small silver coins from his pocket, threw them into the crowd. There was a mad scramble, and in the confusion, he gave an order to the coachman and climbed in. They were off, husband and wife.

Chapter Eighteen

The Houses of Parliament were in session until the beginning of July and the newlyweds were not to leave the capital until it went into recess. Then they would go to Overshott, the family estate in Middlesex. They were therefore now on their way to Shrewsbury House for the wedding breakfast. The ball introducing the new Countess to the *ton* would be in two weeks. In the meantime, according to convention, they would be left alone.

There was silence in the carriage for the first part of the ride. Gradually, though, Louise came to her senses and was just thinking she should say something when her husband (would she ever be able to call him that?) spoke.

"That went off well, I think," he said. "One has heard it all many times before, of course, though it's rather different when it applies to oneself."

"Have you been to a lot of weddings, then? I've only been to one or two." Louise tried to speak calmly.

"Yes, I'm probably the last of my set to get married. Most of my friends succumbed years ago."

His words appealed to her sense of humor. "You make marriage sound like a disease!" she smiled. "Though if you think about it, perhaps it is. The actual joining together part is very short. It's really only a few lines. Like a disease, the initial exposure may be brief but the effects linger on."

He looked at her, and saw the corners of her lips turned up and the humor in her eyes. Her sense of humor was appealing, and she certainly looked much better than usual. He smiled back. "Yes, I chose the word without thinking, but you make me see the justice of it."

So it was in good humor that they arrived at Shrewsbury House. The servants were all ranged outside down the sides of the broad white steps to welcome the bride to her new home. Louise squared her shoulders and looked up at her husband. He took her arm and led her up the steps beside him. Lisle and Mrs. Smith she already knew. Rose was there, of course, but the others, like the people in the church, were a sea of faces.

In a carriage on the opposite side of the street Diane Courtland watched the couple. Even from that distance, the country mouse looked much better than she remembered. She had not, of course, been invited to the wedding breakfast, and she had not dared go to the church. Gareth would have been furious to see her there, and she wasn't ready to break with him just yet. But she couldn't resist driving to Shrewsbury House to catch a glimpse of them. She saw the bride's presentation to the household and ground her teeth. That should have been her! She drove home and, unable to contain her anger and frustration, sat down to write a note to Lord Youngbrough.

The housekeeper took the new Countess upstairs to her rooms and left her to refresh herself. In a few minutes her mother arrived and spent some time walking around the rooms commenting enthusiastically on everything she saw.

"My goodness, Louise," she said, "I am green with envy. I *am* looking forward to staying with you here in London and having many a long cose with you in this pretty boudoir. How fortunate your father made that arrangement with his friend all those years ago! I hope you are truly grateful!"

Before Louise could contemplate either her gratitude or the prospect of this new relationship with her mother, a tap on her door revealed the housekeeper. The guests were arriving and his lordship was waiting.

Louise went down and stood by her new husband's side in the drawing room as the butler announced their guests. She was at first startled and a little embarrassed to see the deep curtsies and bows she received. But she understood. *It's not me*, she said to herself. *I am respected because of my rank. I am the Countess.* She lifted her chin, smiled calmly, and said a few words of welcome to each of them.

Although she was totally unknown to most of the guests, not one considered her an unreasonable choice for the Earl. Her appearance and demeanor were such that they considered her perfectly suitable. She was not beautiful, but her manner and the few words of greeting she quietly gave all the guests showed she was a lady. Like his lordship, they agreed this was the most important qualification in a wife. Besides, he was no oil painting himself.

Louise did her best to remember the guests' names. Her caricaturist's trick of homing in on an unusual feature helped her. Thus Lady Wroxford was *the very narrow nose*, Lord Plimpton *the triple chin*, Mr. Pryce *the tiny feet* and Mrs. Overton *the very large hands*. The honorable Beau Mainwaring wore creaking corsets and his wife had the bright inquisitive eyes of a terrier. Unbidden, a picture of her came into Louise's mind. She would draw her standing on her hind legs, a ruff around her neck, a bow in her hair and her eyes shining as if she were expecting a bone. Louise's own eyes danced with amusement.

She wondered why the Honorable Percy Struthers and his wife Alicia looked at her with vague hostility until the Earl made him known as his second cousin. It was he who had effectively been cut out of the title. As they walked away she heard his sharp-faced wife saying, "She certainly looks pleased with herself. And no wonder, she's fallen into the honey pot. But elegant gown or no, she doesn't bring any beauty into the house. Between the two of them, one wonders what on earth the heir will look like!"

Louise had made much the same comment to her mother weeks ago, but it hurt nonetheless. Her husband must have heard it too, but when she glanced up at him, his face was impassive.

When the stream of entering guests had trickled to nothing, the butler said quietly in her ear, "I believe all the guests are here, my lady. The kitchen is ready. May I announce the Breakfast?"

"Yes, thank you Lisle," she responded at her most formal, and took a deep breath. The first part of the ordeal was over.

Chapter Nineteen

The party trooped into the dining room, the Earl and his Lady first, and the rest according to a ranking both they and Lisle were mysteriously somehow aware of.

Since it was a wedding breakfast, the newlyweds were placed side by side at the head of the table, unlike the rest of their married life when they would sit at either end. The Earl walked Louise to her seat. Since no one could sit before she did, she quickly took her place while he stood beside her until all the other ladies were seated. The gentlemen followed. Footmen moved around filling one of the many wineglasses in front of each place, then, almost as soon as everyone was seated, they had to stand again. His lordship took up the glass and said, "Ladies and gentlemen: His Majesty, the King." Standing, they drank the loyal toast. Then the feast began.

And feast it was. The footmen brought in a seemingly endless stream of dishes. First came two different soups, starting with a thin broth and then a sorrel soup with cream. This was removed by dishes of cod with mushrooms and prawns in pastry baskets. Then a huge haunch of venison was carved at the sideboard, together with several brace of partridges, both having been sent up from Overshott a couple of days before. These were accompanied by roasted root vegetables, pickled beetroot, a dish of stewed apples and three or four meat pies.

The numerous glasses next to the places were filled with a dazzling array of different wines, from pale hocks to deep clarets.

Louise took barely a sip from each, but most of the gentlemen appeared to swallow it down wholesale, and even some of the ladies' cheeks began to grow pink. The disappointed cousins, seated near them at the top of the table, were amongst those who ate and drank everything put in front of them, as if to gobble down as much of the estate as they could. The volume of the conversation at the table, which had started at a genteel level, began to rise.

Louise had no appetite, but covertly watching her husband, she saw he ate well. He drank moderately. At one point, when offered a new wine, he tasted it, shook his head and murmured something to Lisle, who immediately signaled to the footmen standing ready to pour. They all halted. Those carafes disappeared, and others took their place.

Just when Louise thought the meal would go on forever, the table was cleared and the footmen poured champagne. The Earl's best man, who Louise had seen for the first time that morning, proposed a toast to the married couple accompanied by the sort of silly innuendos these occasions usually call for.

Then she and the Earl stood, and two footmen carried in a very tall, tiered cake covered with white frosting. Fully three feet high, it was held between them, and to her immense embarrassment, Louise realized she and her new husband were supposed to kiss over the top of it. For the Earl it was easy enough, but she had to stand on tiptoe and nearly overbalanced. She had to clutch at the sleeve of one of the footmen. Her husband's lips barely brushed hers, but even so, a great surge of emotion welled up in her. An immediate outcry of acclaim and loud applause greeted the kiss and she was glad to be able to sit down while it continued.

The cake was taken away and a collection of sweets arrived: almond tarts, candied nuts, syllabub, and lemon flummery with spun sugar floss, together with a number of cheeses and huge bowls of strawberries. Then, finally, plates of wedding cake were placed in front of the guests. More toasts, congratulations, reminiscences, and increasingly ribald comments from the gentlemen ensued until it became quite rowdy. Louise was wondering how much longer it would go on until she saw her mother looking at her very meaningfully and making a slight upward motion with her chin. She realized it was she who had to bring it to an end. She stood up.

This was a signal for the ladies to leave the gentlemen to their port. The gentlemen all rose as they exited the dining room. Louise went thankfully up to her own rooms while the other ladies were shown upstairs to the bedrooms designated for their use. A general loosening of stays, a powdering of cheeks and a smoothing of hair took place amongst the older ladies, while the younger ones spent their time in a covert examination of their rivals' toilettes, privately finding them all wanting in some particular or other. No one found fault with the bride's appearance, however. "Absolutely lovely gown," was the universal assessment. Louise would have been surprised to know that no one mentioned her plainness.

Chapter Twenty

The bride was glad to regain her own apartment, but she was not long alone, as her mother and the Dowager Countess soon followed her. She was astonished when the Dowager made her a formal curtsey.

"Oh, no, my lady!" she cried.

"Oh yes, my dear," said her husband's grandmother. "You are *my lady* now. It is right and proper for me to make my obeisance to the new Countess. The day will come when you will do as I, and pass the crown, so to speak, to your successor, but in the meantime I wish you every happiness as the Countess of Shrewsbury."

The unreality of the wedding, the welcoming of all those people she did not know, the interminable time at table, on top of a sleepless night both longing for and dreading what was ahead, and now this. It was all too much. Tears filled Louise's eyes.

"I know it all seems strange," said the Dowager, coming to her and taking her hand. "But you will get used to it. I cried my eyes out on my wedding day, too. Did not you, Mrs. Grey?"

In fact, Mrs. Grey had not. She had been aware of her own beauty and had felt all the attention she received perfectly appropriate. Of course, her wedding had not been as grand as this. However, not wishing to reply negatively to the Dowager, she replied, "It's a common reaction, I'm sure. But the delights of being a wife and having your own establishment will soon dry your tears, my dear."

Louise wanted to say that this would never be *her* establishment! She was just one in a long line of wives to the Earls of Shrewsbury. Without her husband's name, she was a nobody. A plain, insignificant nobody. She had to dig her nails into her palms to prevent herself from saying it out loud. But then her natural optimism reasserted itself. She had said she would arrange it, and she would. She smiled, a little tremulously.

"Of course," she said. "You are both so kind. I'm just a little overwrought. If you'll excuse me, I'll just wash my face and hands."

And she went through to her bedroom, where, behind a pretty rose-covered screen, stood a washbasin and jug of water. Having held a cool cloth to her face for a few minutes, she squared her shoulders and looked at her face in the ornately framed mirror.

"You are the Countess," she said sternly to her reflection. "Act like it!"

The three ladies went downstairs to the drawing room, where they were soon met by the others. In due course, the gentlemen arrived. Coffee was served in thimble-sized cups, and there were glasses of dark liquids for the gentlemen and a few of the ladies. But it was clear the festivities were over, and before long, the guests started to depart. Louise found herself being curtseyed to again, but this time she was ready for it. She nodded graciously to everyone, murmured a few words, and very soon they were all gone. Louise's mother left with the Dowager, with whom she was to spend another day or two before returning home.

The newlyweds looked at each other.

"I don't know about you, but I'm glad that's over," said the Earl, "Do you have anything you wish to do now?"

The question caught Louise off guard. Although she had never stopped thinking about that night, what they would do in the afternoon had never occurred to her. She gave a tense little laugh.

"Yes," she replied, too tired to dissemble. "I confess it was a bit of a trial. In fact, if you have no objection, I think I should like to lie down." Then, as her face flamed in embarrassment, "I mean, I'm very weary, I'd like to rest, not...." She couldn't continue.

"Of course not," he said quickly. "Come."

He led her upstairs to her door.

"Shall I have Lisle send your maid?"

"Yes, please." She hesitated. "I can't undo all the buttons you see."

She gestured to her back. For one moment she thought he might offer to do it for her. She tensed, her heart beating fiercely. But he just nodded, bowed, and said, "I hope you are able to get some rest. I'll see you downstairs for dinner."

She watched him go back towards the stairs, not knowing whether to be glad or sorry, then opened the door to her apartment.

Rose was in her own room when the summons came for her to attend her mistress. It was the first time she'd ever had such a space to herself, and she was reveling in it. She'd been astonished when the housekeeper had shown her in.

"Oh!" she said, "is this all for me, then?"

"Of course," replied Mrs. Smith, a little haughtily, "This room has always been kept for her ladyship's dresser. I think you'll find everything here you need, but if something is missing, please let me know."

The room was large enough to contain a long table. This was for the dresser's use in making repairs or alterations to the Countess's garments. Rose didn't know this, and, indeed, had no sewing equipment of her own. She had been used to borrowing from her aunt anything she needed for the minor repairs or darns to Louise's limited wardrobe.

The table was set under a narrow window high in the wall. Once the housekeeper had gone, Rose scrambled on top of it, and by standing on tiptoe was able to see the view. Like all the other servants' quarters, her room was on the top floor of the townhouse, just under the roof, and the window looked out over the chimneypots of London. She wondered where Freddy lived and if he would find her. He had said he would, but the city was so large. Just look at all the rooftops!

"What yer doin' up there?" The maid bringing the message that she was needed downstairs looked up at her in amazement. She was London born and bred, and the chimneypots held no fascination.

"Just lookin' around."

"Well, 'er ladyship is askin' fer yer."

"The Dowager?" Rose was puzzled.

"No, yer ninny. The new one. The new missus."

"Oh, yes, 'course!" Rose looked sheepish. "I'm not used to it yet!"

She went out into the corridor and looked up and down.

"Which way is it?"

The servants' quarters were accessed both by a back staircase leading up from the kitchen and another, hidden behind an unobtrusive door on the middle floor where the main bedrooms were located. This was to be used only when servicing those rooms and was absolutely forbidden to any of the servants without business there. The scullery maids and kitchen boys barely knew of its existence. The girl led her to the door and opened it.

"Down them stairs. There's a door at the bottom."

"Sorry I been so long," said Rose when she finally arrived, a little out of breath, at her mistress's chamber. "It's ever such a big house! I thought her ladyship's one was big, until I saw this. And I got me own room! You should see it! 'Course," she chattered on, "it ain't a patch on this. Your rooms is lovely, Miss, m'lady, I mean."

"Yes, they are," responded her mistress. "It's going to be a change for both of us. I hope you'll be happy here."

"Oh, I will, don't you worry," said Rose blithely.

As she lay down on her bed a few minutes later, her silk wedding gown put carefully away, Louise wondered whether the same could be said for her. But before she had time to think too much about it, fatigue overcame her and she slept.

Chapter Twenty-One

It was late afternoon by the time Louise was awakened by a knock on her door and the entrance of a maid bearing a tea tray. She set it down and lit the candles next to the bed.

"Mr. Lisle said to bring you tea and tell you 'is lordship said 'e would see you at 'alf past seven in the drawing room," she announced. "Dinner is at eight, unless you would like it different," she added, "'e said to say."

"No, please tell him that would be fine." Louise thought for a moment. "Is his lordship downstairs?"

"I don't think so, m'lady. D'you want me to ask Mr. Lisle?"

"No," Louise said quickly. "No. I, er, it's not important," she ended lamely.

The maid curtseyed and left. Louise thankfully drank the tea, and ate one of the little cakes accompanying it. She'd eaten very little at the wedding breakfast and was now quite hungry. But then she remembered how the Dowager had merely tasted the sugar wafers the day she visited her and her mother, and decided that was enough. From now on she was *her ladyship* and her ladyship did not gobble down sweets, no matter how hungry she was.

She slipped out of bed and ran across to the communicating door between her and her husband's rooms. She pressed her ear to it but could hear nothing. As quietly as she could, she turned the knob and opened the door a crack. It was too dark to see anything, but the intense stillness told her the room was empty. She pushed the door fully open and stepped inside. Immediately the same masculine scent as that in the library assailed her nostrils. Her heart beating, she took another step and peered around. There was no one there, or seemingly had been recently; the bedcover was perfectly smooth. Where had her husband been all afternoon, if he wasn't downstairs, and hadn't been here? Surely he could not have gone to the House of Lords on his wedding day?

Louise stepped back and closed the door, undecided what to do next. She went back to the tea tray and, without thinking, ate a second little cake.

For heaven's sake, she told herself angrily when she realized what she was doing. *There are any number of explanations as to where he is. You were fast asleep. What was he supposed to do, wait by your bedside like the prince in the fairytale? Stop eating!*

She went over to the large wardrobe in her room and, apart from her wedding dress, saw her meager array of gowns hung there. She surveyed them: her old brown dress, brought because she had an unaccountable attachment to it, the gold evening gown and yellow day dress her mother had had altered for her, the blue chintz day dress, and a couple of nondescript garments she'd had for ages. Knowing what Véronique had told her, she knew not one of them was becoming, but they were all she had.

In fact, she should order a whole new wardrobe, but she was conflicted. As the Countess of Shrewsbury she knew that being properly gowned and coiffed was important. But as wife to Gareth Wandsworth, it was different. Her husband must take her for what she was. She didn't want to try to capture his interest by wearing expensive gowns in compensation for her lack of beauty. That was ridiculous, anyway. The minute she took off her dress and let her hair down she would be herself: plain Louise Grey. But neither did she want to be the little wife tucked away at home. She wanted him to appreciate her and then, she hoped, love her. How was that to be achieved?

Mulling this over, Louise washed herself in the cool water on the washstand, and shivering slightly, slipped on a clean chemise and petticoat. Then she stepped into the gold evening dress that had been her mother's. It was a testimony to the lack of fit that she could do it up easily behind the neck. She looked at herself in the long mirror on the inside of the wardrobe door. She now saw how it bunched under the arms and made her look shapeless.

And what about her hair? It was still pulled on top of her head, but strands had fallen down. If she took it out, neither she nor Rose would be able to do it up again, so she simply tried to push the errant locks back in place. Tomorrow she would braid it as always.

A pretty ormolu clock in her sitting room told her it was now gone six. She would go downstairs and find something to read. There might be a newspaper in the library.

Chapter Twenty-Two

The landing was quite dark in the late afternoon and a footman was engaged in lighting the candelabra that stood in mirrored alcoves in the walls and down the stairs. He stopped and bowed as Louise walked past. She smiled at him and looked so girlish in her ill-fitting gown and tumble-down hair that he afterwards told his colleagues, "She ain't no beauty, that's fer sure, but she don't hold herself so high she wouldn't give yer the time o'day."

Louise went boldly into the library and found the newspaper next to a leather armchair, where her husband had obviously been reading it. She would have liked to curl up in the same chair surrounded by the delicious scent of leather and old books, but didn't dare to do so. This was his private domain. He'd said he'd meet her in the drawing room, so that's where she went.

She had just sat down when Lisle came in.

"My lady!" he exclaimed. "I had not thought to see you down here so soon, or I would have made sure the room was lit."

Then, seeing the newspaper, he fussed over her, bringing a branched candle holder to a small table next to a chair he thought she would find comfortable.

"I would have brought you the paper, too, my lady, if you had asked me," he said.

Louise smiled up at him. "Thank you, Lisle," she said. "But I'm not accustomed to asking people to do things I can do myself."

If he thought that now she was the Countess of Shrewsbury, she should perhaps expect a little more, he said nothing, except to ask if he could bring her anything else. When she declined, he bowed and left her.

She settled down and was soon immersed in the news of the day. Princess Caroline, long estranged from her husband the Prince Regent, had apparently moved to Italy where she had set up household with a certain Italian gentlemen who was reputed to be more than just her *majordomo*. The Regent himself, it was reported, was spending the summer in Brighton at the palace on the Steyne to which he had added stables built in an ornate Indian style. He had significantly enlarged the palace itself ten years ago and was now considering another extension. He was closeted with an architect called Nash and there was talk of an extravagant design in the Oriental Style.

Then in another article, a self-styled Diplomat asserted that exiling Bonaparte on Elba was too close to home. Hadn't he heard almost immediately of the death of his wife back in May and reportedly locked himself in his room for two days? If news could reach him that fast, he was not far enough away. There were some who claimed he was even now plotting an escape.

Louise was plunged in these and other fascinating pieces of news when she heard a step and a voice in the hall. Evidently the Earl had returned from wherever he had been and Lisle had informed him his wife was awaiting him, for he came into the drawing room, still clad in the same clothes he had worn at the wedding. He appeared to be in a bad mood. His dark brows were drawn together and his face looked even more than usually stern and craggy.

"Louise!" he said. "You're here."

"Yes," she smiled. "Were you expecting someone else?"

"Of course not," he replied, not responding to the humor in her tone. "But I didn't think you'd be downstairs so soon."

He advanced into the room and looked at her narrowly.

"Did you, er, dress for dinner?"

She understood at once that neither her gown nor her coiffure announced that she had, in fact, done so.

"Yes," she replied lightly. "Though I realize it doesn't look much like it."

He drew his brow together again and seemed about to say something, but evidently changed his mind.

"I'll be back in a few minutes. Please ring for Lisle if you desire anything."

"I'm quite happy, thank you. Take your time."

She smiled at him, determined not to be affected by his mood. He nodded briefly and left the room.

He went swiftly upstairs and barked at his valet, a thing so unusual that his man looked at him in surprise. The Earl was a man used to having his own way, but his demands were not excessive. He expected his clothes to be ready when he wanted them, his meals to be hot and on time, and above all, for his horses to be well looked after. He didn't like surprises, but his household was so used to his requirements he didn't encounter any. He rarely had to speak sternly to his staff.

What had put him in his present mood was something he had seen on the way home. After leaving Louise upstairs that afternoon, he had read the newspaper and then wondered what to do. His bride was asleep, and her confusion when she mentioned *lying down* hadn't escaped him. There was no chance of an afternoon dalliance. In fact, he wondered how difficult she was going to be that night when he approached the ticklish question of the consummation of the marriage.

He didn't want go to his club, where everyone knew it was his wedding day and he'd be subjected to salacious conjecture as to why he wasn't at home with his bride. He thought he'd take a look in at Jackson's Boxing Saloon where there was a promising young boxer Jackson had told him he should look at. Glad to have something to do, the Earl rode over there and watched the would-be champions being put through their paces. The young man in question had been everything Jackson had promised, and his lordship had agreed, as he quite often did, to finance his training.

His way home took him past Diane Courtland's little townhouse. He had been both surprised and annoyed to see Denis Youngbrough come down her front steps with a jaunty air and walk down the linkway, swinging his cane with the air of a cat that got the cream. It could mean only one thing. Gareth was half inclined to rein in his horse and go in to have it out with her, but his sense of honor forbade it. He would not visit his mistress on the very day of his wedding.

So he had been simmering with discontent when he arrived home, and to find his wife calmly reading the newspaper in a bunched up gown and her hair all anyhow had not improved his mood. And she hadn't seemed remotely concerned about it. He remembered how she had looked when he met her. She had made no effort then, either. Was that what he had to look forward to? He glowered and drew his brows together so fiercely that his valet began to think he must have offended his master in some way.

"Have I, er, displeased you, my lord?" he asked tentatively.

"What?" The Earl looked at him as if he didn't know what he was talking about, then, realizing what he meant, answered in a softer tone, "No, you fool. You've done nothing. I've had a bit of a disappointment is all."

Chapter Twenty-Three

The grandfather clock in the corner of the drawing room was ringing the half hour when the Earl returned. He had changed into evening clothes. Though they were well tailored, they did nothing to disguise the powerful frame beneath. A swallow-tail coat sat smoothly but not tightly over his wide shoulders; a grey waistcoat covered his broad chest and his snowy white neck cloth glinted with a diamond pin. The black breeches and silk stockings emphasized his muscular thighs and calves in a way that the trousers and boots he wore during the day did not.

He looked slightly less annoyed than before, and Louise was wondering if she dared to ask where he had been during the afternoon, when Lisle came in with a glass and a decanter on his tray. Next to it stood another glass containing a golden liquid.

"Your *fino*, my lord," he announced. "And I have taken the liberty of bringing her ladyship a glass of the *oloroso*. I have found ladies often enjoy it."

He placed the glass and decanter on a small table near the Earl and brought the tray with the fluted glass over to Louise. She took it and sipped. It really was delicious.

"Thank you, Lisle," she said and smiled at him.

"What in God's name was that stuff you tried to serve us all earlier, Lisle?" said her husband abruptly. "I thought I'd ordered the Chambertin, not turpentine."

Lisle's face fell. "I'm sorry, my lord. I opened the bottles you requested but the 1785 Chambertin fell sadly short. I had decanted several bottles two hours earlier but failed to taste it. I take full responsibility for the near-disaster."

"Well, if you were going to poison anyone, I would have hoped it would be my dratted cousin. Pity he didn't drink any."

Lisle gave a small smile. "Quite so, my lord. May I bring you anything else?"

"No."

Then, as the man turned to leave, the Earl added, "Oh, you might give Cook our compliments and tell her she outdid herself today. I fully expect to hear she's been poached away by one of the guests who fell in love with her *cod aux champignons* and offered her twice the wage I pay."

"Your lordship will have your little joke," replied Lisle with another small smile. "You must know Mrs. Bootle will never leave you. When Monsieur Pierre left us in the lurch as he did, you gave her the opportunity to become the only female chef in one of the great houses of London. She will never leave Shrewsbury House."

"That French charlatan! I'd forgotten all about him. Thank God he pushed off. Mrs. Bootle is worth ten of him."

"Indeed, my lord." Lisle bowed and left them.

Louise had been listening to this exchange in surprise. *Little joke*? It was obvious Lisle understood his stern and haughty master, and took no offense at his abrupt, even impolite, way of speaking.

"I feel very guilty," she said. "I didn't go down and thank them after the wedding breakfast. I was just so tired I didn't think. I feel much better now. Thank you for being so understanding, by the way. I hope you had a pleasant afternoon?"

"Moderately so," he responded. Then changed the subject, asking abruptly, "Why were you so tired?"

"I... I...." How could she tell him she'd been awake all the night before worrying about the night ahead? "I suppose I had a lot on my mind." She tried to laugh it off. "It's not every day one gets married."

"Thank God," replied her husband.

"Oh dear, is it already as bad as that?" Louise's ready sense of humor came to the fore.

"Well, it does tend to interfere with one's routine."

This struck her as such an understatement that she went off into a peal of laughter.

The Earl gave a small smile. "I can see that was a ridiculous comment, but I suppose I've become accustomed to living alone."

"And what is your routine? Do debates in the House claim your attention every day?"

But before he could give an answer, Lisle came in to announce that dinner was ready.

Chapter Twenty-Four

The butler led them into the dining room, where the huge table had been re-set for the two of them. Multiple candles had been lit in all the wall alcoves and a many-branched candelabrum stood at each end of the table. Though a number of the leaves had been removed, this was still at least twelve feet long. Though the room was well lit, seated at one end, Louise felt her husband very distant indeed.

The meal was long and complicated. Louise thought Mrs. Bootle must have been planning it for weeks, coming as it did on top of the wedding breakfast. But now she was very hungry and ate with good appetite. After the soup, there were scallop fritters and smoked cod's roe with lemon. These were removed with roast beef, duck with cherries and cutlets of pork. There were pickled cucumbers, apple compote and a mess of leeks in cream. It was all delicious, and because she took very small servings, she was able to do justice to it all.

Once the first pangs of hunger had been assuaged, she looked down the long table and said, "How rude of me to be gobbling down my dinner and making no attempt to pursue our conversation."

"Not at all," answered her husband politely, "I'm glad you are enjoying it." In fact, he liked to see a woman with a good appetite. Most of them seemed to exist on air, eating hardly anything of what was placed before them.

"I asked before about the frequency with which you attend debates in the House," continued Louise. "Forgive me if I seem nosy, but it must be fascinating to be at the center of power like that."

Her husband gave a snort of laughter. "Then you will be surprised to hear that a good deal of the business before the House could hardly be described as pertaining to the center of power. Last week there was a discussion of the problem of people bathing in the Thames, whereby one poor Member declared himself forced to witness public nakedness. The week before we had to vote on the erection of yet another statue in honor of a Major-General who fell in action. I'm sorry for the poor fellow, but if we continue to clutter the metropolis with statues of dead Generals there will soon be no room for living people. Then there are interminable adjournments while different factions get together, or waiting around for the Prince Regent to put in an appearance, which, as likely as not, he fails to do. I try to avoid days when nothing of particular importance appears on the calendar."

"Did you go there this afternoon?"

The question startled him and his eyebrows drew together.

"It's just that you seemed in a bad mood when you returned."

The Earl decided he might as well tell her half the truth. "No. As a matter of fact I went to see a young boxer perform. I like the sport and encourage youngsters when I can."

"And you were disappointed?"

He realized he had painted himself into a corner. Drat the woman! Was he going to have to explain himself like this every day?

"Not exactly, I, er... I usually practice there in the mornings and I missed it today." That was at least true.

"Oh. You like to engage in the sport yourself, not just watch it?"

"Yes, I seem to have a knack for it. I'm an indifferent fencer and a poor shot, so it's a natural choice."

"So part of the routine you talked about is going to this boxing establishment?"

"Yes, Jackson's."

"How lucky to be able to do something one is actually good at! We women are forced to learn to do things for which we have no aptitude whatsoever. I can't sing and I'm a dreadful pianist but oh, the scales I have been made to practice, and the songs I have had to caterwaul! I'm also hopeless at sewing of any sort, and do not even ask me to cover a screen! The only thing I succeed in covering is myself, in glue!"

In spite of his lingering bad mood, her husband was forced to laugh. "But why are you made to do these things?"

"To capture a husband, of course! Our whole education has but one goal, and that is it!"

"I see." The Earl was silent for a moment. "But does it work? Do women capture husbands, as you call it, by such means?"

"But surely," she hesitated, then forced herself to say his name, "Gareth, you are better able to answer that than I! Has any young lady entranced you with her expertise on the pianoforte or delighted you with the elegance of a reticule she fashioned out of pasteboard and lace?"

He laughed again. "No, evidently not, for I never married one of them, and you have just told me you can do none of those things."

"There! It's just as I told my mother. The whole relationship between men and women is based on a tissue of falsehoods! We are told you appreciate abilities that obviously you do not, and you are led to believe we are all naturally talented when in fact we have been subjected to forced labor to achieve even a modicum of excellence!"

They were both smiling when Lisle came back into the dining room and said, "My lady, my lord, the staff would be gratified if you would step into the foyer so that we may add our felicitations to those of your guests earlier. I have taken the liberty of pouring champagne."

In the wide foyer the whole staff was arranged in a semicircle. The women were on one side, from the scullery maid in her blue mob cap and pinafore, to the kitchen and upstairs maids with their white aprons and lace-edged caps. Rose was in her high-throated dress and the housekeeper in her black gown. The men were on the other side, from the leather-aproned boot boy and the grooms from the stables to the liveried footmen and Johnson, his lordship's valet, and Lisle himself in his sober attire. There must have been twenty of them altogether. They all looked at their new mistress and had the same thought. She didn't look like any Lady. Her hair was falling down, her gown was ill-fitting and she was frankly plain. But she was smiling.

Chapter Twenty-Five

In the foyer, Lisle stepped forward and said, "It is the best of occasions when a house welcomes its new Lady. I speak for us all when I say this is a happy home, and we hope and pray your ladyship will be happy in it. My lady, my lord, we offer you our heartiest congratulations on your wedding and wish you a long and fruitful life together. Be assured of our devoted service to that end." He raised his glass, "A toast to Lord and Lady Shrewsbury!"

The staff repeated the toast and drank. Then the Earl said, "Thank you Lisle. I am confident that her ladyship will trust and rely on you all as much as I do. I have instructed my man of business to give you all a week's extra wages this quarter in honor of my marriage and to thank you all for the hard work I know the preparations must have entailed."

There was a murmur of approval. Lisle bowed. "Thank you, my lord." Then to the staff he said, "You may return to your posts."

They dispersed amid bows, curtseys, and chorused good wishes.

"Should I serve tea early, my lord?"

The Earl looked at his wife. "Shall you want tea, Louise?"

Louise was still trying to process this new vision of her husband as a thoughtful and popular employer "Er, no thank you. The dinner was delicious and I shall just run down to thank Mrs. Bootle. Then, then I…." She stopped in confusion. *I expect to be going to bed with you?* What should she say?

But her husband had already turned away. "Then I'll see you back in the drawing room. Thank you, Lisle. We'll ring if we need anything."

Louise walked slowly down the kitchen stairs, glad of the opportunity to regain her composure.

When she came into the busy kitchen all chatter stopped.

"Oh, please carry on," she said. "I just came to thank you, Mrs. Bootle, for the wonderful dinner and the wedding breakfast. I hope everyone down here had a chance to taste some of it. It was the best food I have ever eaten."

They looked at her and had the same thought they'd had upstairs. But they absolved her of her plainness and were inclined to blame Rose. Why hadn't she, so pretty herself, done something to help her mistress?

Mrs. Bootle was astonished that the young bride had come down on her wedding day and immediately became her fervent supporter. "'andsome is as 'andsome does," she said afterwards to Mrs. Smith. "Better than some flibberty-gibbet who don't even know downstairs exists."

Louise made her way back upstairs even more slowly than she had come down, wondering what was going to happen next. She went into the drawing room and found her husband looking at the discarded newspaper.

"So they think Bonaparte is plotting an escape," he said, standing as she came in. "It wouldn't surprise me. For one thing, that new king of theirs seems a poor fellow. The nobles, or such as are left of them, will support him, but the people will want a real leader. Bonaparte, for all his faults, was admirable in many ways."

They both sat down.

"I understand he did a great deal for the education of boys," replied Louise, "but not, unfortunately, of girls."

"Ah, we are back to your hobby-horse. But perhaps now is not the best time to discuss it further."

Her husband looked at her, his hooked nose and craggy features accentuated by the candlelight and his eyebrows drawn together. But he didn't seem annoyed, and Louise remembered what his grandmother had said about his dark look being just a trick he had when he was thinking about something, or hadn't quite made up his mind.

"Look, Louise," he said abruptly. "Let's not beat about the bush. Are you prepared to consummate this marriage? If you'd rather wait, I will fall in with your wishes."

"Oh, no!" She burst out. "I would much rather *not* wait! The contemplation of the event has already given me enough sleepless nights. Let's just get it over with!"

"I'm sorry it appears such a hurdle," he replied a little coldly, "but it is the purpose of the marriage after all."

"Yes," and to herself she added, *That is my whole purpose. I am to be the receptacle of the heir.*

"Then let us, to use your words, get it over with."

They both stood up. Her husband opened the door and led her upstairs.

Chapter Twenty-Six

Forever afterwards, Louise would feel that her wedding night was when she finally knew herself. The instinctive pull she had felt towards her husband from the first moment of their meeting manifested itself in a passion she had never known she had. Before, she had been a plain, introverted maiden, given more to talking to herself than to others, her feelings well under control. But from the moment her husband put his large, warm hand in the small of her back and kissed her, she became another creature. She abandoned all restraint, responding passionately with her whole being. Then during the act itself, a thrill ran through her such as she had never before experienced.

Afterwards, she lay in a glow of well-being, her chest heaving and her heart pounding. Certainly it had been painful for a minute or two, but it was a pain she would willingly experience again for the joy of what followed. Was this what her mother had meant by *sometimes quite pleasant*? What an understatement!

Her husband had been calm and almost business-like at first, but then became as abandoned as she, giving a great groan at the end, before collapsing on top of her. She could feel his heart racing as fast as her own. After a few moments he muttered , "Sorry, I must be suffocating you," and turned onto his back. She wanted to say he wasn't suffocating her at all, that she loved the feeling of his whole body on hers, but she couldn't find the words. They lay quietly next to each other for a while, then he turned and kissed her on the cheek. "Thank you, my dear," he said, and left her.

She fell asleep almost immediately and did not wake until the maid came in with a tray the following morning.

"Beggin' your pardon m'lady, but Cook sent up some muffins, in case you could fancy some. They is ever so good!"

Louise started to sit up, then realized her nightgown was on the floor where she had thrown it the night before. She had desperately wanted to feel her husband's naked skin against her own. She blushed and pulled the sheets across her chest.

When the girl had gone, Louise quickly slipped her nightgown back on and then lay sipping her tea and nibbling a muffin (they *were* very good!) thinking over what had happened. She had become another person: uncontrolled and shameless. Would she have been like that with any man? Is that why girls were continually warned not to allow themselves into compromising situations? Because they would lose all control as soon as a man took them in his arms?

But she knew that could not be so. At school the senior girls had all been in love with a young music master. He was tall and willowy, with fair hair and blue eyes. He looked like a poet. She had pretended to swoon over him like the others, but looking back she knew he had meant nothing to her. She forgot him as soon as he was out of sight. Her husband constantly occupied all her thoughts. Just his presence made her heart beat furiously. She longed to see him again.

For his part, the Earl had returned to his room the night before in something of a daze. Louise's reaction to their lovemaking had both astonished and delighted him. He had never been with a maiden before and her words earlier that day had led him to believe she would be afraid, even tearful. She had talked of sleepless nights worrying about it, but nothing in her demeanor had been fearful. Quite the reverse. She had welcomed and reciprocated his embrace. He fell asleep satisfied, pondering this unexpected outcome.

But the next morning at the boxing saloon he found that his pleasure the night before was two-edged. His reflexes were slower and his normally powerful right jab weaker than usual.

"You're a newly married man, my lord," said Gentleman Jackson after the training bout. "Stands to reason you'd be less aggressive. Been using your energies elsewhere, I daresay."

"Never happened to me before," muttered the Earl.

"But it's different with a wife, like most things," laughed the older man. "We always tell our lads to lay off relations with the old trouble and strife before a fight."

After the dousing with a cold hose that served as the ablutions for young and old, rich and poor alike in the establishment, the Earl rode home in something of a quandary. Was he to lose his abilities every time he spent the night with his wife? That would be a pity. But the contract they had signed had been for only twice a month. That would solve the boxing problem, but, dammit, did he want to be limited like that? Recalling his experience of the night before, it was a difficult choice.

Chapter Twenty-Seven

"Are you expecting his lordship home for luncheon?" Louise asked Lisle later that morning.

"Yes, my lady. He said to expect him."

She tried to appear nonchalant, but her heart leaped.

"Please serve it in the breakfast room. I know he prefers that. And tell me, Lisle, is there a smaller sitting room I could use? The drawing room is beautiful, but it's so vast, I feel quite lost in it."

"Well, my lady, her ladyship the Dowager used to like the small parlor next to the breakfast room, but it was shut up when she left the house. His lordship has never used it, preferring the library. Would you like to see it?"

She hesitated. "Yes, I would, though before using it I think perhaps I should ask his lordship."

"I'll just fetch the key."

When he returned, the butler led her into the breakfast room. To her astonishment, he walked up to the trompe l'oeil wall and fitted the key into a door that was invisible amongst the painted foliage. It swung open and they advanced into a room about the same size as the one they had left. The curtains were drawn over the long windows and it was quite dark. Lisle threw them back, and a cloud of dust danced in the sudden light from the French windows that opened, like those next door, onto the lovely garden. The furniture was shrouded by holland covers, and when she put her hand on something that looked like an armchair, it came back white.

"I'm sorry, my lady," Lisle apologized. "It hasn't been cleaned in many years. No one ever comes in here, you see."

"One can see it's a lovely room, all the same. Thank you for showing me, Lisle. It would be perfect."

Louise could see herself in here, reading with the doors wide open onto the garden, the sound of the fountain in her ears. She reluctantly turned to leave when the wide shoulders of the Earl suddenly blocked the doorway.

"This is where you are!" he said coming into the room. "Good lord, I haven't been here in years."

The surge of emotion caused by the unexpected appearance of her husband, together with the sense she was invading a private space rendered Louise speechless.

"I... I...," she stammered.

Lisle came to her rescue. "Her ladyship was looking for a smaller sitting room. I took the liberty of showing her this."

The room apparently aroused no sentimental memories for him. He answered shortly, "Yes, well, it looks as if it needs a good cleaning. Is luncheon ready?"

Apparently unperturbed by this abrupt reply, Lisle merely bowed, "I'll ask Cook, my lord" and slipped out of the room.

Louise hesitated, unsure of what to do or say next. In spite of the previous night's revelation, or perhaps even because of it, as she dressed that morning she had been even more determined to be her normal self. She had put her hair in its braid and was wearing the shapeless pink dress.

Her plan worked all too well. Looking at her now, her husband could see nothing of the passionate creature who had fascinated him the night before. The twice a month contract suddenly didn't look so unreasonable.

"Good morning, Louise," he said, distantly polite. "I should have said that before, but I was surprised to hear voices coming from in here. I'd forgotten the room existed."

Louise tried to calm the thump of her heart.

"Good morning, Gareth." She hesitated. "I hope you don't mind my being here. It's lovely. I should like to use it, if I may."

If she was hoping for a reminiscence from his childhood, or some sort of remark exposing the heart of the man beneath the frown, she was disappointed.

"Of course," was his only reply.

"Thank you," she said maintaining the same distant politeness as he stepped back to allow her to walk into the breakfast room. "Lunch is to be served in here. In fact, I was hoping we could eat all our meals in here when we are alone. It will make conversation much easier. Is there anything particularly interesting in the newspaper today? I haven't seen it yet."

And as Lisle served their lunch, they talked lightly of this and that, though more than once Louise's lively wit made her husband smile.

Chapter Twenty-Eight

And so passed the period of their honeymoon, if such it could be called. After their wedding night, the Earl made no advances towards his wife. He was polite, even pleasant, but not affectionate. They spent little time together. In the mornings Gareth either exercised his horses or went to the Boxing Saloon. Then he went to the House. It was near the end of the session and the Lords were working longer than usual hours to deal with unfinished business. The married couple would meet at the lunch or dinner table, when they would discuss the daily news or questions raised in Parliament. He talked to her as he would to a colleague.

"I wish Stanhope would know when to shut up," he said one day. "He does tend to let his enthusiasm get the better of him, even when he can see the mood of the House isn't behind him. We've a lot on our plates before recess and his blathering on doesn't help."

"Oh, I rather like people with enthusiasms," said Louise. "Even if they do go on about them. But I can imagine all the Lords are dreaming of sitting in the garden under a tree pretending to read the newspaper and don't want to listen to any of it. I expect you will be happy to get away, too."

"Yes, I will, but I won't be spending much time reading under a tree. There's always a lot to do at Overshott: meetings with the land agent and bailiff, checking on work that has supposedly been carried out. I simply exchange one job for another. The other day one of the Members introduced a Bill in the house aimed at limiting the beggars in the London streets. He seemed to think the only way was to pay them off, and handsomely too. Apparently they earn three shillings a day from begging, so they'd be fools to take less. I thought then that being a beggar sounded better than being an Earl. I should like to be paid for doing nothing."

Louise laughed. "But if you dislike being an Earl, can't you pass the title to your second cousin and his charming wife?"

"Unfortunately, that's not how it works. As long as I'm alive, I can't pass him the title. I'm born with the millstone and only death will release me from it."

Louise looked him in the eyes and said seriously, "If that's true, you must instruct me in what I can do to make the millstone lighter. I would be glad to do it, you know."

"Thank you," he answered with a rueful smile, "but I'm used to it, like a donkey with its burden."

They said no more on the subject, but he found himself thinking of her response. He'd never thought of a wife as a partner.

For Louise the best part of the day was these meal times with her husband. Initially, she longed every night for him to repeat his visit to her bedchamber, but soon realized he was keeping to their contract. Sometimes she would hear his voice and his valet's shortly after she had retired, but more often there would be no sound at all. A few times she had crept to the door between their chambers and listened, then carefully opened it, as she had that first day, but it was empty.

She didn't allow her disappointment to show, but filled her days making every effort to be a cheerful and competent wife. She explored the house, including the shrouded ballroom, and went down to talk to Mrs. Bootle and Mrs. Smith about the arrangements for the upcoming Ball. She spoke a few words with any member of staff she encountered. She wandered around the garden and chatted with the men working there. Soon, familiarity with her appearance meant the staff no longer saw what she looked like, but only how she was, and they appreciated her.

In the mornings she would drink her tea and nibble her muffin in bed before getting up. She would have liked to breakfast with her husband, but thought that, like most men, he probably liked peace and quiet in the mornings. Then, having been down to the kitchens to check on the menus and other arrangements for the day, she would sit down to read the newspaper.

Lisle now had this taken to her sitting room when the Earl left the house. The room had been thoroughly cleaned and with the dust covers off, the furniture was revealed to be comfortable, slightly faded chintz-covered armchairs and a settee. With the French windows open to the summer day, it was perfect. If it was warm enough, she would sit for a while in the arbor, the scent of roses in her nose, watching the play of the fountain.

She knew she must improve her wardrobe and, putting aside her qualms about dressing to attract her husband, visited Véronique to order a number of gowns for different occasions. The modiste had already sketched out what she knew would suit her, and Louise was happy to follow all her proposals. They agreed she would wear her wedding gown for the Dowager's Ball. Most brides did this. She shyly asked the modiste how much the gowns were likely to cost. Her quarterly allowance seemed enormous, but she knew the modiste's creations were far from cheap. The answer made her blink. So she asked Véronique to send each new gown with the bill as soon as it was ready. That way, she could put a stop on the orders if she ran out of money.

For the time being she had only her old clothes, but this turned out to be a blessing in disguise, for it meant that she and Rose could walk out incognito in the afternoons. They would leave the house on foot refusing both footman and carriage, and make their way around the streets. No one knew her, or recognized her in her ugly bonnet and ill-fitting gown. She enjoyed getting to know the area, with its fine homes built in squares around shady gardens where nursemaids walked their often fractious charges.

She found much to amuse her. One day, a clearly aristocratic lady descended from an emblazoned carriage with the head of a yapping pug emerging from her massive bosom. On another, a painted gentleman in bright yellow pantaloons and refulgent top boots tried to mount his horse, but was so tightly corseted that even with the aid of several footmen who attempted to lift, push, and pull him onto the animal, he could not get his leg over the saddle, and in the end had to give up. A carriage was brought round and he left, in no good temper, his exhausted footmen wiping the sweat from their eyes.

The only attention they drew was that of the appreciative eyes directed towards Rose. They were strolling along towards the end of the first week when a good-looking young man lifted his cap in her maid's direction. She slowed her steps and a blush came to her cheek.

"Do you know that young man?" asked Louise.

"No, well, yes, that's to say, 'e delivers the newspaper to the Dowager's 'ouse and I 'ad a few words with him when we was staying there."

"I see. He's nice-looking, I must say."

"Yes," Rose blushed again.

It suddenly occurred to Louise that she had a responsibility for the girl. She knew now how a strong attraction could lead a young woman to act.

"You said he delivers newspapers. Does he deliver ours?"

"No, m'lady, but 'e said as 'ow 'e'd look me up when I got back to Lunnon."

"Then I hope you won't be tempted to do anything... foolish, Rose," she said hesitatingly. "It's hard sometimes when a man is, well, attractive."

"Oh, don't you worry, Miss, I mean m'lady," said Rose stoutly. "I know what they're all after, and they're not gettin' it from me, not without a ring on me finger!"

"Good."

They walked along in silence for a few minutes, then Rose said, "'E's wanting to better 'imself, 'e told me. 'E talks to the newspaper men, seemingly. 'E sold one of them a story."

"A story? What sort of story?"

"I don't rightly know. But 'e got ten shillin's for it!"

Chapter Twenty-Nine

When she returned home after her walk, Louise would usually have tea in what was now known as *her ladyship's sitting room*. She had started doing her caricatures again: the guests at the wedding breakfast, the personalities observed during her walks. She would smile to herself remembering their peculiarities. She kept her portfolio of drawings in her rooms upstairs, and Rose would giggle over them.

"I don't know why, but there's more odd-looking folks in Lunnon than there ever is at 'ome," she observed one day.

"Perhaps you're right. More people with money to indulge their whims, that's certain," Louise responded. "But I think it's also because people live closer together, so we see more in a smaller area. But there are odd characters at home, too. I mean, remember the two Miss Trotters and their hats decorated with the fur and feathers from all their animals?"

"Oh yes! And that time their cat died and they 'ad 'er stuffed and stuck right on top o' one of their bonnets?" Rose gave a hoot of laughter. "Pity you never did a drawing of them!"

About ten days after the wedding, Louise was surprised one afternoon when Lisle came into her sitting room and announced, "The Dowager Countess, Lady Esmé, my lady," and the Earl's grandmother swept in.

"Don't get up, my dear!" she cried as Louise rose, "I should be leaving you in peace, but I wanted to see how final plans are progressing for the Ball."

"Very well, my lady," replied Louise. "I know Mrs. Smith sent the menu and flower choices for your approval, and the musicians and dance master were interviewed and chosen weeks ago. You left me nothing to do except choose the color of the carpet for the front steps. Because it's been so long since a Ball was held here, Mrs. Smith turned out all the old diaries to see what was done in the past. It has always been red, as one might expect, so I left it at that."

She took a breath. "I know it's a little unusual, but I've decided to allow guests access to the back garden. I'm going to have the breakfast room cleared and the door wide open so there will be a clear path to the French windows and the garden. It's so pretty and the evenings are warm. I've spoken with the gardeners and they will be putting lanterns in the trees. I hope you approve."

The Dowager gave a little laugh. "It's your home, my dear, you must do what you like. Moonlight and lanterns? The younger set will adore it! It will be interesting to see how the Mamas deal with the effect it's all bound to have on their daughters!"

"Oh dear, I didn't think of that!"

"Don't worry, Louise. It's a charming idea. I'm all for it! What does Gareth think?"

Louise grimaced. "I haven't asked him. Like you, he told me this is my home and to do as I like. Let's hope he meant it!"

"I'm sure he did. But what is this?"

The Dowager's eye had fallen on a caricature Louise had just completed. It was the comic image of a lady she had observed that afternoon. She was clearly doing her best to hold on to her faded youth. Her improbably yellow hair curled from under a chip bonnet that would have been suitable for a girl just out of school, and the bright red circles on her cheeks demonstrated enthusiasm rather than expertise on the part of whoever applied them. She was very thin; her arms were like sticks and her head bobbed on a neck that looked too narrow to carry it. She was wearing a gown much too young for her, in a fine muslin that was almost transparent in the sunlight. The low neckline revealed a raddled décolleté swathed in row upon row of multicolored beads. She teetered along the linkway carrying a lace parasol. She looked not unlike a marionette and that is how Louise had drawn her, her thin arms held by strings and her rouged-cheeked head nodding above.

Lady Esmé picked up the drawing. She trilled a laugh. "Why! It's Caroline du Bois! It's her to the life. What a silly creature she is, to be sure! You know, she was lovely when she was young, but with the sort of ethereal beauty that doesn't last. She faded before she was thirty, poor thing. Maurice du Bois left her very well provided for and she spends her money trying to regain her youthful looks. The cures that woman has been on, and the diets! I heard she was eating nothing but pickled cabbage at one point. Please, Louise, may I show it to a friend? She was desperately in love with Maurice but Caroline pipped her to the post. She never really got over it. It would do her so much good to see this!"

"Well, yes, of course, though I wouldn't like it to get into this Caroline's hands. I just do them to amuse myself, I don't want to hurt anyone's feelings."

"Don't worry. I won't let it out of my possession!"

At this point, Lisle came in with the tea things. Lady Esmé put the caricature in her reticule and the conversation turned in a different direction.

"You have ordered new gowns, I hope," said the Dowager, looking narrowly at her granddaughter-in-law's ill-fitting garment.

"Yes. Luckily, I am not yet going into society, so my lack of wardrobe has not been an inconvenience. Véronique has promised a day dress and an evening gown this week. She said I should wear my wedding dress at the Ball."

"Quite right. It is truly a beautiful creation. Shall you wear the tiara?"

"I should like to, but neither I nor Rose can manage my hair."

"Then you need a new dresser."

"Oh, no. Rose suits me very well and I like her."

She didn't tell the Dowager about their companionable walks or the shared memories from home that buoyed her up when the situation with her husband preyed on her.

"Then I'll send Booth over on the night of the Ball. Perhaps she can teach young Rose what to do."

That night, Louise lay in bed thinking about the Ball. Her anticipation of the fast-approaching event was one of excitement mixed with dread. Neither the Dowager nor Gareth knew it, but it would be her first. She had been to a few informal routs and small dance-parties while still at school, but her father's death soon after she had come home had prevented her from going to any real Balls.

She had had dancing lessons at school, but most of her experience had been partnering other girls in country dances and Cotillions with set figures. To be sure, they took turns with the dancing master, but he had to be shared amongst a dozen of them. Then, just before Louise left school, a new headmistress had been appointed. She was a very forward-looking individual. It was she who had encouraged the girls to read Mary Wollstonecraft, and even more daringly, she had introduced the Waltz.

Louise had loved it, finding it almost impossible to sit still when the lilting music was playing, but the only man she had ever danced it with was the dancing master. He was a middle-aged, slightly portly gentleman with a large family, deliberately chosen, in fact, because he roused no flutterings in the young maidens' breasts. She now thought if the Earl put his arm around her waist, the hammering of her heart would be loud enough for everyone to hear. And what if she stepped on his toes? She blushed in the darkness of her bedchamber just thinking about it.

Chapter Thirty

But it was the day before the Ball that filled Louise with even greater fear and longing. It was the beginning of the second two-week period of her marriage. It was two weeks and one day since her wedding night. It meant her husband might visit her that night. Of course, it could be any day, but Louise faced it with a barely controlled constant quiver of excitement. She hoped he might say something at lunch, but when she saw him he was even more frowning than usual.

"Has there been a problem in the House?" she asked.

"Some damned fool has told the Prince Regent there's a plan afoot to attack him and now he won't step foot outside the palace. What a mess!"

Louise wanted to ask any number of questions, but seeing his scowl, bit her tongue.

In fact, Gareth was wrestling with the subject of the night ahead too. She would have been both glad and dismayed to know what he was thinking. He was eager to repeat the experience of their wedding night, but his wife's calm, cheerful demeanor since that event had led him to believe she didn't care one way or the other. Then there was the likely dampening effect on his boxing. The more he mulled it over, the more irritated he became. The Prince Regent's movements, or lack of them, were a minor irritant.

So their luncheon ended and they went their separate ways, both dissatisfied.

Louise had wanted to see the sights of London and had dragged Rose to St. Paul's Cathedral and Westminster Abbey, but what the girl really wanted to see was the wild beasts at the Tower of London. Over the years foreign potentates had given gifts of exotic animals to the Crown and they were housed there. To relieve her preoccupations, Louise decided this was the day they would go. Accordingly, when she and Rose went out for their usual walk, she surprised the maid by hailing a hackney to take them there.

The trip took them east, past St. James's Palace, where Louise smiled to herself, imagining the Prince Regent peeping out from behind the curtains for sight of anyone who might be coming to attack him. They passed the enormous and elaborate King's Mews, finally arriving on the bank of the Thames. Small boats and ferries plied their trade here, but as they approached the Tower they could see the massed sails of tall ships clustered close to the bridge. It looked as if one could walk across from ship to ship without touching the water. And one would not want to touch the water, for it stank!

"Pooh!" said Rose, holding her nose. "Fancy living down 'ere! I never smelled anything so bad in me life, not even old man Thomas's pig pens back 'ome!"

It had turned into a very windy day, in fact Louise was worried this weather might continue the next day and spoil her al fresco arrangements for the Ball. They decided that if they were going to get all blown about, they would do it just before going home and visit the inside displays first. These were all Rose could have hoped for. She sighed over the story of the bones of the Little Princes found in the Bloody Tower, and shuddered at the rack and manacles used to extract information or confessions from prisoners in the torture chamber.

"I'd tell 'em anything they wanted to know!" she said. "They wouldn't even 'ave to start!"

After that, the animals seemed somewhat of a let-down. Rose said they looked very much like what she had seen in her books at school. She liked the lions, though, commenting that they didn't look very fierce. "More like big pussy cats," she said.

"I doubt they'd seem like that if you were in the cage with them," Louise laughed. "But let's find a hackney. This wind is blowing me to bits and my hair is all in my face. I must have done my braid looser than usual. Anyway, we should be getting home."

It was quite late by the time they arrived, and the Earl, returning from an afternoon session in the House, was astonished to see what looked like two untidy maidservants descending from a dilapidated hackney carriage in front of Shrewsbury House. They were laughing together at something, and it wasn't until one of them turned to pay the driver that he realized it was his wife. Strands of hair were emerging wildly from a bonnet with a vivid yellow lining that did nothing for her complexion, and the pelisse she was wearing hung off her shoulders. *Good Lord,* he thought. *Is this what she looks like when she goes out? And why didn't she take one of the carriages instead of that atrocious vehicle?*

He hung back until the pair had gained entrance to the house and had time to go upstairs before going in himself.

"I just saw her ladyship descending from the most God-awful vehicle," barked the Earl, handing his caped riding coat and beaver to the butler. "Why didn't she have a carriage?"

"I'm sorry, my lord," came the reply. "She didn't indicate she would be needing one when she went on her walk today."

"I don't like to see her with no protection. Make sure it doesn't happen again."

Not waiting for a response, Gareth took himself upstairs and without knocking, went into his wife's rooms.

Rose had just unbuttoned Louise's old gown and slipped it off her shoulders. It fell in a puddle around her feet as they both stared at the Earl.

He stared back. "I, er, I...."

For a man accustomed to speaking in the House of Lords, words came with unusual difficulty to the Earl as he contemplated his half-clothed wife. Then he collected himself.

"Thank you, er, Rose, isn't it? That will be all."

Rose glanced anxiously at her mistress, who, her face flaming, nodded briefly and stepped out of the gown. Rose scooped it up in a bundle and left.

Chapter Thirty-One

Louise stood there in her petticoat, her hair, which had begun to unravel in earnest from its braid once she took her bonnet off, falling in waves around her face. She was blushing and had the look of a schoolgirl discovered in the middle of a misdeed. She looked adorable.

The Earl swallowed and began again. "I, er, wondered why you didn't use one of our carriages to go wherever it was you went this afternoon. I don't like you to go about unprotected."

"I wasn't unprotected." Louise's blushes faded. She was slightly annoyed by the question. Surely she could travel how she liked. "I had Rose with me. Anyway, how do you know?"

"I saw you paying the driver of that abominable hackney."

"I know, it was awful wasn't it? But it was getting late and it was all I could find at the Tower of London. There are lots of visitors there, you know. They all need hackneys."

"The Tower of London?"

"Yes, Rose wanted to see the animals. Actually, it was quite interesting. Did you know they have a giraffe there?"

"We are getting off the subject. Why did you take a hackney at all?"

Louise looked straight at him. "Because I don't have the wardrobe to be seen in public as the Countess. Dressed as I was, and not using the carriage with your Coat of Arms on it, no one recognized me."

"But why in God's name don't you have the wardrobe?"

"Your grandmother told me we'd be staying quietly at home for two weeks and would receive no invitations. I wanted to order things from the modiste here in London. She made my wedding gown and understands what I need. But I didn't anticipate spending most of my days on my own, and to fill in the time I've been going out incognito on discovery outings with Rose. Anyway, look! There are boxes from the modiste on my bed. They arrived while I was out. I was just getting ready to try things on. That's why I'm...." She gestured at her undressed state.

The Earl was struck by her words. He suddenly realized he'd made no provision for the entertainment of his wife. He had left her, a stranger to London with no acquaintance, entirely to her own devices. He should have done better. He had been so determined that marriage should make no difference to his life, he had paid no attention to what a huge difference it would make to hers.

"You should have said something," he muttered, unaccustomed to being wrong-footed. "I could have arranged... something."

"But you are so busy with your *routine*. And in spite of some of the stories you tell, your work in the House is important. I don't mind looking after myself. But you must see that I could hardly go about as the Countess of Shrewsbury looking as I do!"

"I think you look very nice... like that." The Earl took a step towards her, his eyes on hers. "You are... delightful."

Then he took her in his arms and kissed her.

Louise was completely unprepared for his embrace, and trembled all over.

Her husband drew away. "Don't you like me kissing you?" he frowned.

"Yes, I do! I do like it very much! Oh don't frown!" She put her finger between his eyebrows and smoothed them apart. "I am just so unused to being kissed I don't know what to do."

His brow cleared. "You seemed to know what to do on our wedding night."

"Yes, I did. I don't know how."

"Shall we repeat the performance later?"

He would have liked to have taken her to bed there and then, but he had been brought up to understand the need for regularity in a household that employed a large number of people all dependent on his movements. He could not upset the routine.

"Oh, yes! Please let's!" Then she blushed. "Later, I mean." She, too, understood the need for regularity.

Her husband left, thinking for the first time in his life that he'd like to upset the damned routine.

After some reflection, Louise unpacked the evening gown Véronique had just sent. Her whole body was tingling from her husband's embrace, and she wanted to look her best for him. She put on her new gown. It was of purple silk with a split-front ivory overdress, cut away like two wings beneath the bosom and ending in a short train. The V neckline was cut wider and lower than she was accustomed to, and the swell of her breasts was revealed. She was doubtful about this, but when she looked at her reflection in the mirror, she saw Véronique was right. It was perfect, cut neither too high nor too low. She had loosened her hair from what was left of the braid and even with it down, the shape of the bodice made her neck longer and her bearing somehow more regal.

"It's really lovely, m'lady," said Rose, who had returned after a suitable interval. "I don't know why you've never worn that color before. It do look a treat on you."

"I suppose I've always thought of purple for widows," said Louise, "but with the ivory overdress it doesn't look widow-y at all!"

After struggling to gather her mistress's loose hair on the top of her head and having it cascade down the minute she took her hand off it, Rose said in exasperation, "Why don't I just make one long braid as usual and pin it around your head like a snake? That might work."

It did. The braid formed a sort of crown that had the effect, like the V-neck of the gown, of lengthening Louise's neck.

"I wish I had some earrings," she said. "Véronique spoke of simple drops, but I don't have any, simple or otherwise."

But when she went downstairs for dinner, her husband didn't appear to think anything was lacking. His eyes brightened as he saw her.

"The new gown is very becoming, Louise," he said. "Véronique certainly knows her stuff."

Louise was surprised. "Thank you. You know her well enough to recognize her work?"

He hesitated. "Er… yes, she has been making my grandmother's gowns this age."

He didn't mention that he had frequently paid the exorbitant price of the modiste's creations for his *inamorata*.

They spoke rather little at dinner, both contemplating the night ahead. When Lisle cleared the last of the dishes and brought in his lordship's port, Gareth said, "No tea tonight, Lisle, her ladyship is retiring early."

Louise took the hint and went upstairs. After her gown was removed, she said, "Thank you, Rose. You may leave now. I, er, I want to try on the other things Véronique sent, so I shall stay in my petticoat."

"But don't you want me t' stay and 'elp you?"

"No, thank you. I may be some time and it's getting late. It's best you go to bed."

When her husband came to her a short while later, Louise was in her petticoat brushing out her hair. He understood, and his eyes narrowed in appreciation.

For them both it was even better than their wedding night.

Chapter Thirty-Two

It was a long time before Gareth left Louise, and both of them slept late the day of the Ball. When he finally arose, the Earl thought it was just as well he had not planned to go to Jackson's that morning. His level of vigor would definitely have been impaired. He breakfasted and went to the library to read the newspaper and escape the activity that was engulfing the house.

It was already like a beehive. Footmen were bringing down chairs that had been stored under sheets in the attic since the last Ball and the maids were swarming over them with dusters. There would be over a hundred people there, and sooner or later, they would all need to sit. Lisle was supervising the lowering of the chandeliers so the candles could be replaced. *Every candle in the house must be new!* was the Dowager's dictum. Between the chandeliers, the wall sconces, and the candelabra in the public rooms, in the foyer, up the stairs, in the ballroom, the billiard room, the card room and the bedrooms prepared for the guests' comfort, hundreds of new candles were being put in place.

Mrs. Smith was taking delivery of huge bouquets of flowers and disposing them in enormous vases throughout the house. The boot boy, watching them disappearing upstairs wondered aloud if there was a single *flah* left in *Lunnon*. Mrs. Bootle and her assistants had already been working for days preparing foodstuffs that could be made in advance, but today the kitchen would be in constant activity from dawn until after the last guests left.

The supper would be made up of foods that guests could eat with their plates on their laps, or at least not at the dining table, where the buffet would be laid. Pastry cases had been made the day before, but today they would be filled or stuffed: pork pies, fish pies, lobster patties, leek custards, mushroom tarts, and cheese flans. Fritters would be made at the last minute to be brought upstairs piping hot. Little cakes had to be iced, pretty strawberry tarts filled, creams whipped, fresh fruit placed artistically in dishes, and nuts and bonbons piled in bowls. And then there was the white soup to be served at the end of the Ball — gallons of it. That would be the signal for the remaining guests (and the number of guests remaining was an indication of the success of the Ball) to go home and leave the hosts in peace. Louise had already agreed with Mrs. Smith that lunch for herself and the Earl would be a cold collation. Cook had enough to do.

Louise awoke with an enormous sense of well-being. She and her husband had crossed some sort of frontier the night before and for the first time she really felt like his wife. Today she would be at his side, being introduced to the best and brightest of the *ton*. She would wear her wedding gown, which she knew became her. She had never been so happy in her life.

She dressed in one of her old gowns and went downstairs around mid-morning to join in the sea of activity. She dealt with an argument in the garden where the footmen had brought chairs outside, making holes in the sanded footpaths and placing them just where they would get in the way. The gardeners were steaming. These ardent protectors of the shrubs and flowers also had a thousand good reasons why everywhere she wished to place the lanterns would not work.

Then she relieved a harassed Mrs. Smith who was dealing with a crying chambermaid. The girl had broken a glass globe on one of the candelabra and was wailing that it shouldn't come out of 'er wages. It were 'Arry the footman's fault because 'e'd put his 'and where he shouldn't just as she was dusting it. The Countess reassured the girl that no one would be charged for the broken globe and listened to the affronted footman who said 'e never put 'is 'and nowhere. Why would 'e touch a girl like that silly Molly when 'e was walkin' out with someone much better?

Then it became apparent that some of the lilies the Dowager had ordered for the flower arrangements were dropping yellow pollen on the polished furniture surfaces or worse, on the Aubusson rugs, and staining them. Louise gave the crying chambermaid a pair of nail scissors and instructed her to remove the yellow pollen stamens from all the lilies. The tricky work needed concentration, so, before long, her tears dried up and the girl worked with a will, her tongue sticking out.

Louise sat down with relief to lunch with her husband, a yellow smudge on her cheek, her quickly-made braid unraveling and a general air of dishevelment.

"You may frown," she said to Gareth, who had drawn his brows together when he saw her, "when you've been closeted quietly in the library all morning!"

"I wasn't frowning," he responded. "I was just wondering why you have yellow paint on your face. And I may have been closeted, but I've made my contribution to the proceedings by tasting every one of the wines Lisle plans on serving this evening. His confidence has been undermined by the Chambertin fiasco at our wedding breakfast. It was vital work!"

They did not linger long at lunch because Louise knew the table was to be removed to make the way open into the garden.

"Good Lord!" said her husband, "I'm glad we don't have to get married and hold a wedding Ball more than once. It's a plague, with all the furniture being carried in and out like dead bodies! Neither the house nor I may ever recover!"

"You don't seem to have a very favorable notion of marriage in general," replied Louise with a laugh. "That's the second time you've compared it to a disease!"

"Yes," his craggy cheeks broke into a smile. "But one I'm finding has some unexpectedly pleasant side effects."

Louise's cheeks flamed. To cool them, she stepped out into the garden. The wind had died down and it was lovely. Proud to show off their abilities, the gardeners had perfected every inch. There were shady spots with welcoming chairs and flower beds in full bloom around each bend in the smoothed path. The fountain was playing musically in the sunlight, the arbor bench had been decorated with pretty cushions, courtesy of Mrs. Smith, and colorful paper lanterns hung from every available branch. She clapped her hands and called to her husband to come and see.

"Look what wonderful work the men have done, Gareth," she said. "It's a perfect spot for you to recover from the ills of marriage!"

Though mystified by her words, the gardeners were more than gratified by the compliment. The Earl smiled, put his arm around her waist and kissed her cheek. "Lovely," he said. He seemed about to say more, but then stopped. "But you are busy. We can talk later."

Chapter Thirty-Three

Louise's mother arrived shortly after lunch and Louise spent the rest of the afternoon showing her around before finally persuading her to take a rest in the room prepared for her.

"My goodness, Louise," she said. "I never knew you to be such an attentive hostess."

Her mother looked in appreciation at her bedchamber. The furniture was glowing, the bedlinen crisp with recent ironing, the filmy curtains that draped the open window moving gently in the afternoon breeze.

"I cannot pretend to have done a tenth of it," responded her daughter. "Mrs. Smith is a marvel. She pretends to be asking me what to do but is actually telling me what needs to be done. I'm so lucky to have her. And, of course, the Dowager is the actual hostess. It is she who sent out all the invitations, ordered the flowers, interviewed the musicians — everything. She must have been a wonderful hostess in her day."

But Mrs. Grey's eye had fallen on something else.

"New candles here as well!" she said admiringly. "I noticed them throughout the house. I'd hate to have to pay the bill!"

"It was the Dowager who ordained we should have all fresh candles too," said Louise. "I must say, I wouldn't have thought of it, but I can see an important occasion like this is not a moment to be a nipcheese."

If that was a hint, it fell on deaf ears.

"I wish you would tell Mrs. Smith to give me some of the partially burned ones when I go," said her mother. "New candles are always such an expense!"

"Oh, mother! Surely that isn't necessary."

But Mrs. Grey, thinking of the cost of her new ballgown, thought it was, and determined to speak to the housekeeper herself if her daughter would not.

Leaving her, Louise went to lie down herself. She was feeling quite worn out and wanted to recruit her strength. It would be a long evening, and perhaps even another long night. She was hopeful she could persuade her husband to forget the contract for once. He had said they would talk later. She lay in dreamy contemplation of that pleasurable possibility until she fell asleep.

The Ball was to begin at nine. The Earl dined at his club, Louise having said Mrs. Bootle was too busy to make dinner for them on top of everything else. When he returned the excitement in the house was palpable, though the scurrying housemaids and footmen were no longer visible. In fact, they were having their supper in the kitchen, talking as excitedly about the Ball as if they were going themselves.

The footmen would be on the upper floors, of course, serving the wine, clearing and replacing empty glasses, and then bringing up the supper dishes. They would also make sure the candles were not guttering or dropping wax, though this was a very unlikely eventuality, since the Dowager had ordered nothing but the very best beeswax. They would all be wearing their finest livery: buttons shining, shoes polished, not a hair out of place. But the only way the maids would see anything was to creep upstairs to see the ladies in their gowns and glittering jewels, and watch the glorious sight of all the dancers. Rose was in a fever of excitement. She had never been anywhere near a fashionable Ball before. Helping to dress her mistress for such a splendid event was the high point of her existence.

After a cold collation to satisfy them until supper at about eleven that night, Louise and her mother both retired to prepare themselves. With the help of several housemaids, Rose and Wilkins — Mrs. Grey's dresser who had of course come with her — carried up ewers of hot water to their mistresses and the lengthy process began.

At least, for Mrs. Grey it was lengthy. She had been lovely in her youth and was still a very pretty lady, but it must be said that her looks were now enhanced by Wilkins' subtle application of powders and colors. Her dark hair, too, was now naturally not quite the color it appeared, and its fullness had to be carefully maintained by the expedient of inserting beneath the elaborate top curls a cushion of hair carefully gathered every day from her hairbrush. Her figure had grown more opulent over the years and was now restrained by a corset laced over her chemise.

It was therefore some time before she could step into her gown and the full effect of the efforts appreciated. But the gown, in the yellow silk that so became her but which she failed to see was quite the wrong color for her daughter, fell elegantly to her slippers from beneath her generous bosom. Only the strictest critic might have said the puff sleeves were perhaps too young for her, but no fault could be found with the matching long gloves and filmy shawl placed delicately over her shoulders by the attentive Wilkins. She wore a fine diamond parure consisting of a necklace, earrings and a very pretty clasp that held a yellow plume to the side of her curls. Her reflection told her that handsome though the tonnish London ladies might be, she would hold her own with the best of them.

Louise's preparations were of a different nature altogether. Never wearing either powder or paint and needing no corset, she was quickly ready and sitting in her petticoat at her dressing table, after a knock, the Dowager and Booth came into her room. Rose was brushing out her disheveled braid.

"The house looks splendid, my dear," said Lady Esmé after a greeting. "Mrs. Smith told me about the trouble you had with the lilies. How stupid of Wolframs to send ones with stamens like that! I shall certainly complain. But your solution was ingenious! And the garden! It will be a fairy land when the lanterns are lit. I just hope they won't all go up in flames and set fire to us all!"

Louise laughed. "The same thought occurred to me. I've set one of the footmen on to supervising them constantly, so I hope not!"

"Perhaps the flames of passion aroused by a summer night under fairy-lit trees we talked about before will be equally restrained by the presence of a hovering footman, though the way young girls carry on these days, I doubt it!"

Like women throughout the ages, the Dowager felt that compared to when she was a girl, the license afforded to young people was scandalous in the extreme. But the remark didn't seem unreasonable to Louise. Goodness knows how she would have reacted if she had felt the flames of passion she experienced with her husband in a candle-lit summer garden or anywhere else. She doubted whether she would have been restrained by a hovering footman. She smiled to herself.

"Booth is here to do your hair, if you are ready," said the Dowager. She looked critically at Rose who, feeling herself inadequate in the presence of her ladyship and her haughty dresser was being more than usually clumsy with Louise's hair. She quickly stepped aside and Booth took over. In no time the coiffure was complete and the tiara in place. Louise stepped into her gown and was soon ready. The longest part of the process was doing up all the pearl buttons down the back.

The Dowager handed Louise her fan, which she slipped over her wrist, and a tiny reticule that contained nothing more than a slip of a handkerchief, a paper of pins, and a small pencil. "Gentlemen often find they have nothing with which to write on one's dance card, my dear," she explained. "So irritating if it is someone with whom you wish to dance, though of course very convenient if it's someone you wish to avoid. It's best to be prepared. The same goes for the pins. You've no idea how easy it is for one's train to be ripped. A clumsy oaf stumbles on it, or it gets caught in a chair leg. Why, I've even known a jealous rival to deliberately step on the train of a competitor! The pins are for emergencies, but it's best to keep the train looped on your wrist as much as possible after you've made your entrance. It's bound to be a dreadful squeeze. Not a single invitation was refused."

Before Louise could comment, there was another knock at the door and the Earl came in.

Chapter Thirty-Four

In a dark long-tailed coat with a white waistcoat and satin breeches, the Earl was dressed with perfect propriety. But as always, his muscular shoulders and broad chest were not made for formal dress. His tailor had done his best, but it was impossible to make him look other than what he was: a man better suited to the boxing ring than the ballroom.

But to Louise he looked wonderful. She would have run to him and thrown her arms around his neck had there not been other people in the room. As it was, she just rose with a smile. The two dressers curtseyed and left the room.

Gareth kissed his grandmother's cheek with a greeting then went up to his wife. "Gran told me the other day you have no jewelry, Louise," he said, "so I brought these from the bank vault."

The inevitable protest came from the Dowager. "How many times have I asked you not to call me that, Gareth. Louise, please don't listen to him!"

In fact, Louise wasn't listening. She had opened the proffered square box and was stammering, "Oh!"

Inside lay a pair of diamond drop earrings with a matching bracelet. They were of an old-fashioned design, but the brilliant stones were set in a rose gold that glowed at its heart.

"They're lovely! Thank you, Gareth!"

She knew he didn't like gushing females, but she couldn't stop herself. She ran to him and stood on tiptoe to kiss his cheek.

"There is a necklace that goes with it, but I thought it too large for your, er, neck," he said. "You will have to come with me to the vault and look at all the family jewels. There may be some pieces you can use, though they are in the taste of a different era. My mother didn't wear them, or at least, she took none to China. I suppose we should be glad, or we would have lost them all."

There was a moment of silence, then the Dowager said, "You made a good choice, Gareth. You're right about the necklace. It would never do, but the earrings will be perfect. I'm not sure, though, that the bracelet will look to advantage with the long sleeves of that gown. It would be better over gloves."

"I think it's beautiful and I'm going to wear it anyway," said Louise, putting it around her wrist and struggling with the clasp.

"Allow me." The Earl took her hand and turned it over, doing up the bracelet. His warm hand on her wrist made her pulse race. She looked up into his eyes. They were deep, dark, and inscrutable.

"Thank you." she smiled up at him, and saw a look come into them that made her tremble.

Her heart beating, she went back to her mirror and with shaking fingers screwed the earrings onto her lobes.

"Turn them till they pinch, then loosen a quarter turn," instructed the Dowager. "You don't want to lose them."

The Earl shifted from one foot to the other and then said abruptly, "I think I'll go down and make sure Lisle isn't going to poison us with the wine." He bowed slightly to the ladies and left.

"What was that about?" the Dowager looked at Louise enquiringly. She explained and Lady Esmé laughed.

They walked along to collect Mrs. Grey and the three ladies went downstairs. Louise reflected ruefully that now she had not only a mother but a grandmother who was far better looking than she. Her ladyship was dressed in her favorite lavender, but her gown was trimmed with fully six inches of white lace along the bottom and around the sleeves. It matched the frivolous scrap of lace she was wearing as a cap on her gold and silver hair. Louise looked at her, thinking how youthful and pretty she looked. But Véronique had said no lace, frills, or furbelows for her. So that was that.

The ladies walked around downstairs. The public rooms looked beautiful, the candles lit, the flowers perfuming the air. A row of footmen stood on either side of the top steps outside and into the hall. They would accompany the guests upstairs and hand them over to Lisle who would announce them at the ballroom entrance. The Earl and Countess would receive them as they passed into the room.

Louise took her mother and grandmother-in-law into the garden. The sun was setting and the men were lighting the candles. The effect was magical. Even the working men, who usually hailed each other heartily, spoke in hushed tones.

"Thank you, my dear," whispered the Dowager with a choke in her voice. "It does my heart so much good to see the old place with a mistress who truly appreciates it." She took the tiny handkerchief from her reticule and dabbed her eyes with it. Louise squeezed her arm.

"I really do understand the responsibility and the honor of my position," she said quietly. "I promise I will always do my best for the family and the Earl."

"There you are," said Gareth, walking towards them and breaking the silence. "We'd best go up, Louise, the carriages are beginning to arrive."

The Countess took her husband's arm and together they mounted the stairs to receive their guests.

Chapter Thirty-Five

The ballroom was almost full when Louise heard Lisle intone, "The Honorable Denis Youngbrough and Mrs. Diane Courtland." She felt her husband stiffen and turned enquiringly towards him. He was bowing over the hand of a voluptuous dark-haired beauty. She was not in her first youth but had a lovely complexion, green eyes, and trim waist. He muttered a few words Louise could not catch, and then the newcomer was in front of her, curtseying low. As she sank down, Louise was treated to a view of her full bosom, enhanced by swansdown that fluttered alluringly around the décolleté. She was wearing a beautiful emerald necklace with matching earrings. The gown was the one Diane had been ordering from Véronique's the day she had seen the future Countess and declared her a country mouse. The jewels were presents from the Earl.

Based on Diane's gossiped assessment, word had gone around that the Earl of Shrewsbury was marrying a country mouse of no distinction or beauty. She was clearly just a well-born vessel for the future heir. Guests had come to the Ball expecting a nobody, and were therefore surprised at being welcomed by a self-possessed, calmly quiet and beautifully-gowned young woman. She was no beauty, to be sure, but she was certainly not undistinguished.

"La belle Courtland was obviously just jealous," whispered one matron to another. "*Au fait de beauté*, the wife's not a patch on Diane, but she don't disgrace him."

"No indeed," responded the other, *sotto voce*, "She seems most ladylike, and that gown is a triumph!"

Diane's first inkling that she had been mistaken was when she had glimpsed the bride from across the street. Now, close up, she had the distinct impression the new Countess was considerably more than she had bargained for.

Louise, not knowing who she was addressing, smiled and said, "What a very beautiful gown! How well it becomes you, Mrs. Courtland."

Diane could detect no trace of irony in this speech and her ladyship's smile was entirely without guile. She didn't know what to think. To cover her confusion, she said, "Thank you. But yours must be the most beautiful one here tonight, I think." Then she stepped away to allow her cavalier Youngbrough to bow over their hostess's hand.

When the couple walked away, Louise turned to her husband.

"You seemed alarmed just as Mrs. Courtland arrived. Is there a problem?"

"Er, no. Not at all. Er," he hesitated, "I'm just tired of standing here. I could wish Grandmother had invited fewer people."

Louise laughed. "It is a crush. She said it would be. But the line of arrivals has gone now. I think we could have the dancing begin, don't you? Lisle will come to get us if more guests arrive."

At a sign from Louise, the musicians drew their musical selection to a close and struck up for the first dance: as always, *La Belle Assemblée*. This began with lines of ladies and gentlemen facing each other on either side of the dance floor, but ended up with them dancing down the room side by side with their partners in one or two long lines depending on the number of participants. It was always a lovely sight to see the toilettes of all the ladies, with their jewels, their tiaras, their plumes, and their colorful gowns.

The maids crept upstairs to see it, amongst them Rose, who had never seen anything like it. She was proud of her mistress in the center of the front row, but her eye was also caught by a pretty lady with a mass of floating stuff around her bosom. Now, that was a gown to sigh over!

La Belle Assemblée was also an opportunity for the host and hostess to dance with all the other pairs, as well as for gentlemen to ogle all the women and for ladies to signal their availability for future dances by coy peeps and smiles at partners they desired. Louise wanted only to dance with her husband, but at the end of La Belle Assemblée he muttered he should look into the card and billiard rooms.

"But will you at least sign my card for the first waltz?" she said. "Look, it's the dance after next. That is, I didn't even ask you — do you waltz?"

"Of course. And I'd be delighted."

"You might not say that if I tread on your toes! But please let me tread on yours before I tread on anyone else's!"

He smiled at that. "Certainly. My toes are at your service."

He took her card and the pencil she provided him with, for, of course, the Dowager had been right and he didn't have one, and scrawled *Shrewsbury* in the appropriate space. Then he kissed her cheek and left.

Diane, watching jealously from across the room, saw the smile and the kiss and determined to have it out with him. He had said their arrangement would not change, but he hadn't been near her since his wedding. Youngbrough was well and truly hooked, but he didn't give her the thrill Shrewsbury did. He had been useful, though. It was he who had enabled her to come to the Ball; she hadn't been invited, needless to say. He had received an invitation because his grandmother was a friend of the Dowager, and Diane had persuaded him to take her. Gareth had been shocked and the

Dowager had looked daggers at her, but everyone was too well bred to make a fuss. She knew they would be.

Louise was solicited for the next dance by the very good-looking Bernie Smithers, a self-professed poet who deplored his prosaic name. He looked the part, though, with wavy blond hair that fell across his brow until in desperation he pushed it into wild curls when a word or image wouldn't come. Just down from Oxford, he too was invited because his grandmother was a friend of the Dowager. The truth was, Lady Esmé loved to be amongst young people, and Balls were one of the few opportunities to be so these days. She had invited an equal number of young ladies, but the poet wasn't interested in them. He had been struck by the Countess's appearance when he arrived. Her ivory slimness reminded him of a naiad. He could imagine her tiptoe on a lily pad. Louise had to smother a laugh when he told her this, for she wasn't keen on the idea of open air bathing, and as for balancing on a lily pad, she could only imagine what a ridiculous sight she would be.

But she was so kind to him and talked so encouragingly about his poetry that he clung to her side when the dance was over and only with the greatest reluctance relinquished her to her husband for the waltz. Seeing her in the arms of the ape-like Earl offended his very soul.

For his part, Gareth had been surprised to see the handsome youngster evidently so taken with his wife. He experienced an odd sense of possessiveness. He would have recognized it as jealousy, had he ever been jealous of anyone in his life before.

Louise was oblivious to all this in the pleasure of waltzing with her husband. His firm hand in the small of her back thrilled her. In spite of his bulk, he was light on his feet and danced well. She wanted it to last forever.

"My toes are completely unscathed," he said at the end. "You dance delightfully. In fact, let me quickly write my name against the last waltz before young Smithers does."

"Oh, he's so funny! Not meaning to be, of course. He said I was like a water nymph! And truthfully, I dislike open water!"

"What? Have you never been sea-bathing?"

"No, and I don't care to!"

"Hmm…, I think we should go to Brighton and have you give it a try. I think you'd find it exhilarating."

"Well, if I'm to be a naiad, I suppose I must, though I'm afraid I should be more like a flounder!"

They both laughed and the sound reached Diane's ears. It caused her to narrow her eyes with determination. In the event, the Earl forgot to write his name against the last waltz with his wife, an omission he was later to regret.

Chapter Thirty-Six

Diane watched Gareth leave his wife and make his way across the room. She intercepted him before he got to his destination.

"I have to talk to you," she said urgently, drawing him into the shadows at the corner of the room.

"I don't think we have anything to say, Diane," he replied. "You made your choice."

"What can you mean?"

"You didn't wait long. I saw Youngbrough leaving your house on my wedding day."

"Impossible!"

"If you say so. I'm not going to stand here arguing with you. I am due to dance with my mother-in-law."

"Mother-in-law!" spat Diane, and couldn't stop herself adding, "Is she as lovely as her daughter?"

"You've said enough."

The Earl began to walk away. Diane clutched at his sleeve.

"Meet me in the garden when supper is announced. Everyone will go inside and it will be empty. Do it, Gareth, or I'll make such a fuss the old tabbies will have gossip for weeks!"

He sighed. "Very well, but it will be for the last time."

He walked away without looking back.

The crowd was such that Louise did not see her husband in conversation with the pretty lady whose gown she had admired. Hardly anyone did. But the few who observed it were not shocked.

Everyone knew about Shrewsbury and Diane Courtland, though they were surprised he should be *en tête à tête* with her at the Ball thrown to introduce his wife.

"I wouldn't have thought him so loose in the haft," remarked one gentleman to another.

"No, and his wife seems a good sort. Spoke very kindly to us when we came in. M' wife appreciated it."

They shook their heads and, as gentlemen will, dismissed it from their minds.

Louise was busy until supper, talking with her guests between being solicited for very dance. At that point she went quickly down into the dining room to see that everything was in order. It was. She silently blessed Mrs. Smith and the kitchen staff. People came in to fill their plates and sat at the many chairs ranged around the sides of the room. As those filled, she told puzzled-looking guests where other chairs had been set. Gareth did not come in and she wondered where he was. She knew he had dined early and must be hungry.

She herself was too keyed up to eat anything, and she was very hot. It was a pleasant summer night, not overly warm, but the many candles and the heat of all the dancers had caused the temperature to rise uncomfortably in the ballroom. Ladies were vigorously plying their fans, and the men were running their fingers around wilting collars. She beckoned Lisle over.

"I want the windows of the ballroom opened while the guests are at supper. Please bring one of the footmen up to help."

The heat in the long room was stifling. Louise went to one of the far windows overlooking the garden at the back of the house, and was just about to raise the sash when, looking down, she recognized the shapely figure of Diane Courtland hurrying down one of the candle-lit paths. A moment later, the unmistakable form of her husband followed.

Without thinking, she left the window and ran down the stairs. In the foyer, she was stopped by guests with a kind word here, an enquiry there, and then, to her extreme frustration, by Lisle who touched her arm.

"I cannot find his lordship to ask the question," he said, "or I would not bother you, my lady. But we are out of the Hock in the dining room. Alas, there is no more of the Niersteiner in the Cellar. I am proposing to open the Ausbruch if you permit."

Louise knew nothing about wine, and at that moment cared less. "Please do as you see fit, Lisle," she said. "I'm sure his lordship would approve."

Finally, she was able to get to the breakfast room, slip through the open doors and out into the garden. She followed the path, her slippers making no sound on the packed sand. She came around a bend in the path as it skirted the side of the fountain and stopped next to one of the larger trees. There, at the end of a side alley, stood Diane and her husband. The woman's hands were clutching the lapels of his coat, and her face was turned up to his. It was too dark to see her expression or his, but the intimacy of the moment was unmistakable.

Gareth had reluctantly found Diane a few minutes before and had drawn her onto the shadowy path.

"Gary, dearest," she had said, turning her wide eyes up to his. "You know Youngbrough is nothing to me. How can you think I would entertain him in preference to yourself?"

"The evidence of my own eyes, Diane," he replied coldly. "I saw him leaving your house and he's going about looking like the cock of the dunghill. Don't tell me he hasn't enjoyed your ample favors."

"Only because he implored me so. I was sorry for him. He means nothing to me."

"Then I'm sorry for you. But as I said, you made your choice and now I'm making mine. Don't cry over spilt milk. You got the emeralds you wanted."

She reached up and grasped the lapels of his coat.

"It's not the emeralds I wanted, it was you! You said your marriage would make no difference, but it has!"

She looked into his face. "Don't tell me you've fallen in love with that plain wife of yours!"

"I shall not now, or ever, discuss my feelings towards my wife with you, Diane."

With the splash of the fountain behind her, Louise could hear nothing of what they were saying. She stood stock still, her heart thumping. It was suddenly all so clear. Her mother had agreed that her husband most likely had an *inamorata*. All the fashionable gentlemen did. And this Diane Courtland obviously was her husband's. He must have been with her all those times she hadn't heard him go to bed. He had stiffened when Lisle introduced her and here he was, gazing down into her eyes. With a stifled sob, she watched him bring up his hands to cover Diane's, and unable to watch more, ran blindly back up the path.

It was a pity she hadn't waited another moment. She would have seen her husband remove Diane's hands from his lapels, push them to her sides and shake his head in a decided negative.

She ran into a dark corner of the garden and fell to her knees. From somewhere the scent of evening primroses came to her nose. For ever after she would associate that sweet perfume with great sorrow. She wept with her knuckles pushed into her mouth to prevent her sobs. In her misery she didn't see the shape of her husband stride purposefully up the path and into the house, nor, a few minutes later, that of Diane slowly follow.

She didn't know how long she was there, but she gradually realized she could stay no longer. She was the Countess. She had to do her duty. She crept to the fountain and dipped her tiny lace-edged handkerchief into the cool water. She put it over her eyes for a few moments then opened the fan on her wrist and plied it vigorously in front of her face. She thought for a moment, then walked boldly back into the house with the handkerchief over her eyes.

"My lady!" Lisle abandoned his stately tread and almost ran to her. "Whatever is the matter? May I help you?"

"No, Lisle," she managed a small laugh. "It was so hot, I went outside to cool down. In the dark I walked into the branch of a tree and stung my eyes. It made me cry. But I shall be fine presently. Oh dear! Look at my gown! I stumbled and fell. So silly!"

This was said in a loud enough voice for bystanders to hear, and within moments word had spread that her ladyship had injured her eyes in the garden. No one doubted the veracity of her tale, a couple of the old tabbies shaking their heads and remarking that's what happened when one allowed people to roam around outside in the dark.

Mrs. Grey tried to make Louise go to her room to rest until her eyes were less red, but received the response, overheard by a number of others, "Don't fuss, Mama. I was not pretty before, and red eyes can hardly make a difference. The second half of the Ball is about to begin and I'm only sorry my poor partners will have an even worse fright to dance with."

So saying, her head held high, the Countess remounted the stairs to the ballroom.

Chapter Thirty-Seven

Afterwards, Louise never knew how she managed to appear natural for the rest of that dreadful Ball. She was besieged by curious ladies and chivalrous gentlemen but told the same tale of the accident in the garden. One good outcome was that her dance card filled rapidly with sympathetic partners so when the Earl came to claim the last waltz, she was able to deny him. Before supper she had been jealously keeping it for him, but she was now glad to allow the poet to lead her to the floor. He stayed glued to her side whenever she wasn't dancing, determined to protect his nymph from more attacks by tree branches or anything else. By degrees her eyes returned to normal, and though her gown was still soiled around the knees, she looked much as she had at the beginning of the evening. If her conversation was a little more brittle and her smile a little less frequent, no one noticed it.

By any standard, the Ball was a huge success. The white soup was served at two in the morning and most of the guests were still there to enjoy it. The young people had taken full advantage of the freedom of the candle-lit garden; the married women had found congenial dancing partners other than their spouses; the older women had gossiped all evening, minutely observing the two former groups through their lorgnettes and prophesying no good outcome, and the gentlemen had enjoyed billiards and cards accompanied by the product of his lordship's excellent cellars.

The Dowager had had a wonderful evening with old friends in her former home, enjoying all of its benefits and none of its responsibilities. Mrs. Grey had not sat out a dance, and had had more than one gentleman tell her she must no longer hide away her beauty in the countryside. She was forming plans of asking her son-in-law to find a house for her (just a small one, of course) in the capital. It was only for the host and hostess that the Ball had been a disaster.

The Earl's evening had been ruined less by Diane than by seeing his wife in the arms of another man. He didn't know why this should irritate him so much, but as the night wore on his scowl deepened. For Louise, the evening had destroyed her whole happiness. With their shared jokes and conversation of the past two weeks, her initial purely physical attraction to the Earl had blossomed into real love. And she had thought, especially after the night before, that he might be beginning to love her too. Then this! To see him looking into the eyes of another woman and to know he had been intimate with her all along, simply broke her heart. How foolish she was! To think any man could love her: ugly, uninteresting, dull Louise Grey.

When all the guests had gone, she mechanically thanked Lisle and the footmen, then went down to the kitchens to do the same to Mrs. Smith, Mrs. Bootle, and the rest of the staff. It was due to them, she said, that the Ball had been a triumph.

The Dowager had left earlier in the evening, and Mrs. Grey had already climbed the stairs to her bedchamber. Louise didn't know where her husband was. He had been there by her side to bow and thank the guests as they left, but then he had disappeared. She had bid Denis Youngbrough goodnight, and not knowing of the liaison between him and Diane Courtland, had wondered why he looked so disconsolate. But as far as she knew, Diane was still there. She could only assume Gareth was somewhere with her.

Tears came to her eyes as she slowly went upstairs. Rose was waiting for her, full of the sights of the Ball, but Louise cut her off, saying she was tired, her eyes hurt and she just wanted to get into bed.

"What a shame you soiled your gown when you fell in the garden m'lady," said Rose, holding it up.

"It doesn't matter. I shall never wear it again," Louise replied. "Just throw it away."

Rose opened her eyes wide. "Throw it away? Oh, I couldn't, not for fifty pounds, m'lady."

She folded the maligned garment carefully and put it aside.

"If you don't throw it away, I shall," said Louise fiercely. "I never want to see it again. Now just take off this stupid tiara, brush my hair and leave me alone."

She had never spoken to the girl like this before, and Rose was taken aback. But, she reasoned as she quietly did as she was told, perhaps milady was increasing already. That would explain it.

Louise tied on her nightcap, climbed into bed and was about to put out the candle when there was a brief knock at the communicating door and the Earl walked in.

"Oh, er, you're already in bed." He looked uncomfortable, shifting from one foot to the other. "I... er, look, Louise, I've been wanting to talk to you all day, but you've been so busy and then your mother arrived, and then... well, I tried to see you but you were asleep. But you must be tired now, and no wonder, so I'll see you tomorrow."

Louise could see he was out of sorts and clearly needed some word of encouragement. But her husband was the last person she wanted to talk to, so she said nothing.

He hesitated a moment, then said, "Well, good night. I hope you sleep well. You deserve it. The Ball was a huge success. Thank you."

She still didn't say a word. He turned and left.

Chapter Thirty-Eight

Louise passed a dreadful night, unable to dismiss the vision of Diane and her husband in the garden, and constantly thinking and re-thinking what his words had meant. What did he want to talk to her about? As dawn broke she entirely gave up trying to sleep and lay rigidly on her back, deciding what to do.

In the end it was this: she would simply say as little as possible. *Least said, soonest mended* was one of her old Nanny's favorite dictums. She would say nothing about what she had seen in the garden. There would be no recrimination, no scene.

But the easy intimacy with her husband was over. She would be the woman he had apparently wanted to marry: cool, unremarkable, and reserved. She would appear on his arm in public and play the part to perfection. Both at home and abroad she would be pleasant but distant. She reversed her earlier decision to just be herself. She had wanted him to love her as she was, but since that was obviously impossible, she would be *her ladyship* at all times. She would simply be the Countess. Louise Grey would disappear.

Tears came back to her eyes as she thought all this, and at some moments her heart was so full she felt it would explode from her chest, but by degrees she calmed herself and set her jaw. Other society women must live like this. She could, too.

Having made this decision, she lay in a doze. Around midmorning a maid appeared with tea and muffins. She drank the tea gratefully and having eaten nothing since lunch the day before, gobbled down two muffins. When she remembered how she had told herself a lady did not behave like that, she defiantly ate another.

She was still in bed when her husband's characteristic short knock sounded at the communicating door. She snatched off her night cap and sat up.

"Good morning, my dear," he said, and her heart thumped. He had never called her that before. "I hope you slept well?"

"Very well," she lied, and then, politely, "and you?"

"Like the proverbial log. My God! I thought the Ball would never end. I was wanting my bed hours before the last guests left."

And who were you wanting in it with you? The thought came unbidden.

He pulled next to the bed one of the gold spindle-backed chairs her room was well provided with and sat on it. It creaked.

"These damned chairs! They were never made for anyone like me. In fact, I don't know who they were made for, but every house I've ever been in has them."

Including Diane Courtland's, I collect, came the unbidden voice, but she still said nothing.

He seemed not to know how to continue and for a moment there was complete silence.

"I told you I wanted to speak to you yesterday and never got the chance," he said, finally. "What I wanted to say, er, ask you was..., well, to speak plainly, would you would be prepared to ignore the, er, conjugal visits contract we signed?"

Whatever Louise had thought he might want to talk about, it was not this. Her heart rose and for a moment she wanted to shout *Yes! I would! I would give anything to be rid of the contract!* But the voice inside her immediately quelled her. *Why? So that you could have both of us any time you wanted?*

"No," she heard her voice say calmly. "I would not be prepared to do that."

He stared at her. "No?" He sounded disbelieving. "You're sure?"

"Quite sure."

"But I thought…." His voice trailed off. Then he began again, in a different tone. "But I was obviously mistaken. I'm sorry to have importuned you."

He stood, replaced the chair, gave a slight bow, and left the room.

Louise fell onto her pillow and tried to control herself. If only she hadn't seen what she had seen in the garden! If he had asked her that same question before, her heart would have been filled with joy! Try as she would to stop them, tears came to her eyes, and with her pillow stuffed against her mouth to prevent any sound, she sobbed as if her heart would break.

Chapter Thirty-Nine

Gareth Wandsworth returned to his bedchamber, his temper rising. What was the matter with the woman? He would have sworn her answer to that question would be an enthusiastic yes. He was sure she enjoyed their coupling as much as he did. No one could be that good an actress. Then he thought about his wife's attitude. She was usually smiling and talkative. Last night and this morning she had answered practically in monosyllables. Why? Could she be overtired from the damned Ball? Could it be her time of the month? If so, why the hell didn't she just say that instead of that complete negative?

Between Diane throwing herself at him last night and Louise utterly rejecting him this morning, he was sick of women. They were nothing but a damned nuisance. When you wanted them they played coy, and when you didn't they were only too keen. Well, the devil take them both.

He strode downstairs, barked at Lisle for his cloak and hat, said curtly, "I won't be in for luncheon," and left. He went to his club where he proceeded to gamble ferociously and lose a great deal of money. Since this behavior was so unlike him, his colleagues rightly surmised he had wife trouble. They had all been there and the only thing that surprised them was that it was so soon.

Louise consumed a solitary meal, grateful not to have to make polite conversation with anyone.

The doorbell rang constantly with deliveries of invitations, notes, flowers, and small gifts of thanks. She listlessly arranged the flowers around the rooms and sent the boxes of sweetmeats and bonbons down for the servants. Amongst the offerings was a poem from Bertie Smithers. Beautifully lettered on parchment tied with an ivory ribbon, it read:

A naiad she, whose mark is naught
Upon the water gliding,
But on my heart the print she made
Will be forever biding.

She couldn't help smiling at the unlikely image of herself gliding on water. Under normal circumstances she would have shared the verse with her husband and they would have chuckled over it together. She had to blink back tears. Those days of easy camaraderie were over.

At tea-time the Dowager and her mother arrived, eager to talk over the triumph of the ball.

"The gowns! The parures! I've never seen such a sight," sighed her mother. "And who was that woman wearing the gown with the swansdown? She looked beautiful!"

The Dowager had seen Diane, of course, and had deliberately snubbed her. How dared she come! Now she simply said, "Oh, no one of any account. She's one of the women who are always on the fringes of the *ton*. Apparently she inveigled the boy Youngbrough to bring her. He'd better be careful. She'll snap him up in one bite!"

Then she deftly turned the subject. "I've been giving the matter of your hair some thought, Louise. I see you are back into your braid today. I suppose it's well enough for indoors, though you must know it doesn't really become you."

"So I've told her again and again," chimed in her mother, "but it's no use."

"I can't do anything else and neither can Rose," said Louise defensively. "And I do not wish to replace Rose. She and I deal well together."

"So you've said," answered Lady Esmé, "and I'm not proposing you get rid of her. But Booth has a niece who wants to be a dresser. Apparently she's quite good. If Booth says she is, she must be. Anyway, I propose sending her to you. If you like what she does, she can stay here. An extra maid is always useful, anyway, and she's a quiet, well-behaved girl. She can be your personal maid, or, better still, Rose can be your personal maid and this girl Susan can be your dresser. After all, Rose has no qualifications for the job apart from a pretty face and a willing nature."

"Yes, I'm afraid that's so," said Mrs. Grey. "But she's niece to my own treasure Wilkins and I didn't have the heart to refuse her. These women with their nieces!"

Louise was too miserable to enter into any protracted discussion on the relative merits of dressers and quietly agreed with the Dowager. "Please send her over tomorrow," she said quietly, "I'll talk to Rose."

"It's obvious you're overtired, my dear," said the Dowager, looking at her narrowly. "We'll be off."

"And I shall say goodbye, Louise," said her mother. "As you know, I'm leaving the day after tomorrow and her ladyship and I have been invited to tea at Lady March's tomorrow, so I shan't see you again. I daresay you'll be at Overshott soon, so I hope to receive an invitation there."

"Of course, Mama," said Louise mechanically. She embraced both women and walked them to the door.

Chapter Forty

Louise tiredly changed into her purple silk for dinner, though it caused her a pang when she remembered the first time she wore it. She was in the drawing room when her husband came home, and the formality of it helped her maintain a distance when he came in for his pre-dinner sherry. She did not ask where he had been and he did not say. His temper had not been improved by his losses that afternoon and he wasn't sorry when she still appeared less than usually chatty.

When she did speak, though, he was surprised by her formality.

"My lord," she said, "we received a number of notes and gifts of thanks this afternoon, as well as numerous invitations," she said. "I imagine you wish me to answer them?"

"If you want to. Or I can get my secretary to do it."

"By no means. I consider it one of my duties. I shall place them on your desk on the library when I have done so."

"Very well."

Their conversation at dinner was equally detached. Gareth couldn't understand it, but decided Louise was like all other women: given to odd moods and fancies. It was best not to engage them when they were like that. He concentrated on his dinner. The meals they served in his club were at most times indifferent but on occasion, and today had been one of them, positively poor. That's why he almost always lunched at home. He had left nearly all of it on his plate. So now he ate with a good appetite. Louise touched practically nothing: everything she put in her mouth tasted like ashes. Watching her husband, she had to clench her jaw in the effort not to cry out *How can you sit with me and eat like that when you know how poorly you have behaved? Have you no conscience?*

When Lisle came in with the port, Louise left the table and went immediately up to her rooms to finish a caricature she had begun that afternoon. It was of Diane Courtland. It showed her with an exaggeratedly large bosom, tiny waist and an enormous necklace and earrings. Her mouth was screwed into an avaricious bud that made her look positively ugly, but it was unmistakably Diane.

"I saw that lady," said Rose, when she came in later to help her mistress prepare for bed. "She 'ad all that floaty stuff on 'er gown. What was it?"

"I couldn't tell you," said Louise, not wanting to pursue the conversation.

"Ever so pretty she was. You didn't draw her looking very nice, though. Don't you like her?"

"It's nothing to do with liking or not liking. I don't know her. I told you, the caricatures are just for fun. They make me laugh."

"They is usually quite funny," said Rose, "but that one's a bit mean, really."

Louise laughed off the remark as she put the picture in the portfolio, but she knew Rose was right. It was mean.

Finding his wife had disappeared into her apartment, the Earl took himself off to a disreputable inn deep in the Tothill Fields where he watched a boxing match more remarkable for its violence than its science. He was well known at that location, and the pickpockets usually left him alone. Tonight, however, a newcomer saw him as an easy mark as he leaned his broad shoulders against a post, apparently lost in the back and forth of the bout. But his lordship was awake on all counts. When the man, feigning drunkenness, bumped into him with a slurred *beggin' yer pardon, yer honor*, he spun him around, forced open his hand from which he took his wallet, and dealt him a right that sent him sprawling on the packed earth floor. That made him feel better than he had all day. So much better, in fact, that he peeled off a note and sent it fluttering into the man's face. The thief had lost consciousness for a moment and came to with the money falling on him from above. He thought for a second he'd died and was in paradise.

"You're lucky you put me in a good mood," said the Earl. "But don't ever take me for a flat again."

He went home, washed the blood off his knuckles, fell into bed and slept like a baby. His conscience bothered him not at all.

Chapter Forty-One

The Dowager had been right: the period of peace and quiet for the newlyweds was over. In the next week they had invitations to a musical soirée, a select dinner party at Lady Pevensey's and a card party. The week after, there were two balls, one at Almack's for which the Patronesses had sent vouchers. Other routs, ridottos, picnics, parties, and more balls followed.

Louise had already made the decision to accept all the invitations. It would mean in the evenings she and her husband would be more out than in. That suited her, as she would have to spend even less time alone with him. But this plan would necessitate very many more gowns than she had anticipated.

Accordingly, she made a list of the affairs she had to attend and sent them to Véronique. She begged her to make up as a matter of urgency as many gowns as she thought she would need. She would pay extra for expedited delivery.

The Earl frowned at the stack of invitations his wife had accepted on their behalf, but didn't say anything. Had it been up to him, he would have put most of them in the rubbish, but she was new to London and even the most hackneyed entertainment must seem exciting to her. He was disappointed she was still treating him with great distance, talking little and apparently avoiding him whenever she could. But having decided that this was part of the female condition, he shrugged and got on with his life.

He spent long days in the House where there was a great deal to do in the fortnight before the end of the session. On the rare occasion they were at home in the evening, Louise excused herself immediately after dinner and he took himself off to his club. Being married was proving to have as little impact on his life as he had hoped. Why, then, was he dissatisfied?

The first event they attended as man and wife was a musical evening. Gareth detested this form of entertainment and the invitation was one he most certainly would have consigned to the waste-bin. Nevertheless, he resigned himself to an excruciating evening in the supremely uncomfortable gold spindle-backed chairs he hated.

Louise wore the becoming purple and lace evening gown. She hadn't worn it yet outside the home so no one had seen it, and her hair was arranged elegantly.

The Dowager had been as good as her word, and the girl Susan had arrived. There was a moment of confusion at table in the servants' hall because Rose and she were in the same position. But Susan immediately said, "No, Rose, you've been with 'er ladyship longer and you should go above me."

With that, their friendship was cemented.

Susan was as unlike Rose as could be imagined: tall and thin, her scraped back hair and high-necked black gown making her look more than her eighteen years. However, she proved to be more than equal to Louise's unruly curls. She soon had them elegantly pinned on the top of her mistress's head with side curls over her ears.

The soprano sang with more emotion than accuracy and her figure, which was so corseted that it looked as if her bosom were being presented on a shelf, wobbled like a blancmange on the high notes. In spite of the sorrow in her heart, Louise had to bite her lip not to smile. She glanced sideways at her husband to see if he showed any sign of amusement, but his gaze was fixed impassively ahead.

The emotional gap between them was beginning to weigh heavily on her and she longed for someone to laugh with. She had not considered how lonely she would be in her detachment. The first two weeks of her marriage now seemed like halcyon days. She sometimes wished she had not discovered the truth about her husband. Then she would have gladly accepted a change in the infamous contract and been happy in her ignorance. But, she chided herself, it was much better she know the truth. Ignorance was *not* bliss.

She was spending hours in her rooms adding to her collection of caricatures. She realized her unhappiness was making her images darker. She drew them with an uncompromising pencil and though they were funny, they were wickedly so.

At supper after the concert, she exchanged a few commonplaces with her husband before enacting the Perfect Countess, smiling gently and engaging in a quiet conversation with Mr. Rutherford, the somewhat older gentleman on her other side. She gave him her full attention, speaking softly and without coquetry.

"'Pon my word," he remarked later in his club, "Gary Wandsworth has done all right for himself with that Louise Grey."

"Bit of a plain Jane, ain't she? Or at least so I hear."

"Perhaps, can't say I noticed. She's a good kind of girl. Talked sensibly, none of that giggling they go in for. Well informed too. We talked about stuff in the newspaper."

"I never heard old Gary going in for a woman like that. The article he used to have on his arm probably never read anything more than the label on a hatbox."

The select dinner at Lady Pevensey's confirmed Louise's reputation. A new evening gown in a shimmering gold had arrived just that morning. Like her wedding dress, its apparent simplicity belied the excellent cut. Her hair, with which Susan had once more performed miracles, was this time pinned up and threaded with a gold ribbon. She wore no jewelry and looked elegant without ostentation.

On that occasion, she engaged Lord Veness, a grouchy, taciturn gentleman who was generally only invited because his wife was a leader of the ton and it was social suicide to ignore her. He addressed himself with dislike to his plate, for his grouchiness was brought on by chronic dyspepsia, and he had an abhorrence of rich food.

Louise saw immediately what the problem was and made delicate inquiries as to his health. Like most people with constant discomfort, he was only too pleased to reveal the source of his suffering. Louise commiserated with such attentiveness that, though she herself enjoyed perfect health and could eat anything she chose, her partner felt he had found an ally. Lady Veness was astonished to see him actually smile at the new Countess. He certainly did not find her plain. In fact, if asked, he would have said she was a damned fine woman.

Chapter Forty-Two

The next invitation was to Lady Whitlow's dinner and card party. On their way there in the carriage Louise said, "My lord, (she no longer called him Gareth), I hope you understand I know the rudiments of whist, but I am by no means an expert player. I shall not be at all offended if you prefer to partner someone else."

She was hoping not to have to partner her husband. It was so much easier when she wasn't near him. The truth was, she had played cards a good deal at school. The new head teacher had encouraged it as an excellent training in mathematics. As she put it, *use your brain, girls. You'll find it's for more than working out whether you can afford a new bonnet.* They had learned loo, whist, and piquet. Louise was quick and had a good memory. She proved to have some talent for cards, and when she played it with her school friends usually won. They only played for buttons, for the girls were not allowed to bet real money, but she enjoyed it very much.

But her husband was confident in his own ability. "So long as you know the rudiments," he said. "I am sure we can manage between us. Just remember that if I lead a card it's either because I have no more in that suit and therefore can trump it or I have a number of high cards in it and can win on points. In either case, when you get the chance, lead the suit back to me."

Since this was elementary, she didn't need the instruction and therefore merely nodded.

After dinner, the guests went into the card room, where tables were set with their names. Louise saw at once she had been placed to partner her husband. When the first rubber began and he led her a heart, she deliberately led him back a diamond. When he could not stop himself from drawing his brows together with impatience, she said quietly, "Oh, I'm so sorry. I played that badly, didn't I?"

The Earl nodded, still frowning. The rubber continued, with Louise making one mistake after another and at the end they were significantly down.

"I thought you said you knew the rudiments of the game, Louise," said her husband, "but I think you exaggerated."

Lord Veness and his lady were their opponents. His lordship, who had been her admirer since the dinner party, quickly responded, "Don't be like that, Shrewsbury! We all make mistakes. Her ladyship is just beginning. Tell you what, let's switch partners." He addressed his wife, "You don't mind, do you, my dear?"

She did not. She was a keen player and felt herself equal to the Earl.

During the next rubber the Countess appeared to have learned her lesson, for she played without error. She and her new partner won.

"See, I told you she was just beginning," said Lord Veness, pleased to think he had not only brought out Louise's abilities by his generosity but also beaten Shrewsbury, who was known to hate losing.

The third and deciding rubber was played in concentrated silence. Louise clinched the win with a finesse that no one expected, least of all her husband. Her partner crowed with delight and congratulated her for her cleverness.

"But it was pure chance," said Louise untruthfully, "I really didn't know what I was doing. But I did enjoy playing with you, Lord Veness. Thank you."

The Earl took his lady home feeling he had somehow shown himself in a bad light. He had been unfriendly towards his wife and had seen another man bring out the best in her. Illogically, he blamed her for placing him in that position.

The ball at Almack's was even worse. The Earl had studiously avoided the place for years. He hated having to wear the knee breeches and silk stocking that were *de rigeur*. They certainly did no justice to his thick, muscular legs. And in his opinion, the damned *chapeau bras* they were forced to carry under the arm made them look like generals looking for work when the war was over. He also hated the low-stakes card games and the insipid refreshments. You couldn't get a decent glass of wine and all they gave you to eat was stale cake!

But his wife had received vouchers from the patronesses and it would have been the height of disrespect not to go. She was as well dressed as he had come to expect. These days even when at home she always appeared perfectly turned out. Ironically, there were times he missed the old brown gown.

For this occasion, Veronique had sent her a lilac silk ballgown that appeared simplicity itself. It had short puff sleeves and the hallmark V neckline. It fit narrowly over the bodice, but from just below the shoulder blades at the back there was a deep inverted pleat. Circling the gown under the bosom there were three rows of narrow pleats, then the silk fell in a sheer line to just below the knees where more matching rows of narrow pleats added both interest and weight, so the extra material provided by the back pleat swung out elegantly as she danced. There was no train. This was deliberate on Véronique's part, for she had heard the Almack's balls were a terrible crush and gowns with trains were constantly being ripped. The modiste sent over-the-elbow matching gloves. Louise clasped her diamond bracelet over her left arm and wore the matching earrings.

Amid an array of elaborate gowns with ruffles, lace, ribbons, fringe, gimp, and cord, its simple elegance stood out like a swan amongst peacocks.

She had no lack of gentlemen signing her dance card, and her husband was lucky to put his name to anything. The poet Bernie Smithers was there and literally ran to her side. He signed up for the first country dance. Louise was surprised. She expected him to want a waltz, which Almack's had recently allowed into its hallowed portals.

The reason soon became obvious. He had chosen the country dance because it lasted much longer than the waltz, and he wanted not to dance, but to sit and talk with her. He led her to a secluded bench.

"Thank you for the pretty verse you sent," she said lightly. "I'm flattered you see me in such a light."

"You are an angel!" he declared emotionally, and would have taken her hand, had she let him. "But that scribble was nothing! Let me tell you about my new oeuvre!"

She agreed, knowing that the dissertation could only last as long as the dance.

He needed no further encouragement. He first gave her a lecture on poetic forms, declaring at length that the Elegy was the finest, which is why he had chosen it. It exactly suited his mood, with its sense of loss and glories past.

"*Who would not sing for Lycidas?*" He quoted with affecting sorrow, "*... he knew/Himself to sing, and build the lofty rhyme.* Ah! The sublime Milton."

In fact, Louise knew those lines, because while her mother might deplore the freedom with which the young ladies discussed unmentionable topics, her school had provided her with a very good education. She was therefore able to respond intelligently.

Young Bernie then went on to some of his own poetry, which, truthfully, she found very derivative.

"Who would not mourn the loss," he intoned,
"Of France's flower'd youth,
Its hope betrayed and freedom gone,
In bloody wounds and anguish borne?"

For, of course, many were declaring the ideals of the French Revolution were now lost.

"Do you think, then, the French people have lost all the freedoms they fought so hard to gain?" asked Louise.

This led to another lecture, to which she listened as attentively as she could until the final chords of the country dance sounded. In fact, she was covertly looking to see if Diane Courtland was there. She was not. The lofty morals of the Patronesses would never have permitted it.

Mr. Smithers was forced to relinquish Louise to the next gentleman, and since there were no other dances left on her card, he soon took his leave. He couldn't bear to watch her with other men, and turned an even more envious eye on her husband. What had Gareth Wandsworth done to deserve such a jewel for a wife, except have a title and be as rich as Croesus? Damn him.

The Earl observed her tête à tête with the poet and the fact that she was constantly solicited for the dances. Her card had quickly filled and he had been unable to procure a waltz with her. He watched her through narrowed eyes as she twirled around smiling at her cavalier, her beautiful gown swinging out behind her. He could not even bring her a glass of lemonade during the breaks, for she was well supplied by other gentlemen. The fact she had done nothing to which he could take exception did nothing to quell his mounting ire. And when she answered his remarks with polite distance on their way home in the carriage, his black looks and scowl would have alarmed anyone. But she wasn't looking at him.

Chapter Forty-Three

As the days passed, Louise's initial sorrow was replaced by a sense of the injustice of her situation. She too became more and more angry. To be the wife her husband wanted, she had completely changed her way of life and even her appearance. And what had he given up? Nothing. He was continuing to visit his lady-love, for that was how she interpreted his after-dinner disappearances, while she did all she could to keep his home running smoothly and appear in public as the elegant Countess. The more she reflected on these injustices, the angrier she became, until she decided she would make him pay. She would make him see she was not to be the mouse at home while he played with the cat abroad.

Véronique had by now sent her a number of gowns, day dresses, evening and ballgowns and even a gown to wear when carriage riding in the park. The Earl had thought she might enjoy this, but when he asked her to accompany him, she politely refused. The reality was that with her emotions roiling she did not think she could sit close to him alone for so long without exploding, but she told him it was because she had nothing to wear. The park was well known for being an unofficial fashion parade and she did not want to appear without the appropriate apparel.

"Order something, then," he said. "Have them send me the bill."

After some thought, she ordered the carriage dress and told Véronique to send the bills for *all* her new gowns to her husband. She could have paid for some of them herself, but why should she?

Let him pay, she thought savagely. *He wants an elegant wife. It's up to him to afford it.*

The Earl was increasingly annoyed that while his wife was pleasant and smiling to everyone else, to him she was merely coolly polite. His temper was not improved when the third fortnight of their marriage began and he declared his intention of visiting her. She refused him.

"As I recall," she said calmly, "the contract said on *dates mutually agreeable*. This date is not agreeable to me. I prefer to wait."

He scowled with frustration, but would not let his anger show.

"Very well," he said. "Perhaps you would be good enough to let me know which date is agreeable. Until then, I shall importune you no further."

Now, when he saw the eye-wateringly high bill for his wife's gowns, his brows rose.

"Goddam it!" he swore. "So I am to have all of the disadvantages of being a married man and none of the advantages!"

His anger led him to mention the bill to Louise, something he would never normally have even considered.

"I received a large bill from your dressmaker. Have you nothing left of your allowance?"

"Yes, I have, but you said to send the bills to you."

He racked his brain. "When did I say that?"

"When you told me to order a carriage dress."

"As I recall, we talked only of that specific item."

"Oh? Is that what you meant? I misunderstood. I'm so sorry. Would you like me to give you what I have?" Louise feigned surprise.

The Earl would have died before accepting money from his wife.

"Of course not. It's of no matter. I'll pay the bill. But perhaps you will have the goodness to warn me in future when I am to expect such an outlay."

"Yes, my lord."

But things were to go from bad to worse.

Chapter Forty-Four

They had received an invitation from Lord and Lady Barnstable to a supper party with cards. Louise was surprised, for generally a card party was offered after a dinner. This seemed very paltry.

"Oh," explained the Dowager when Louise mentioned it, "Everyone knows Lord Barnstable is all but done up and his poor lady can't afford to give a dinner party. The tradespeople won't extend them credit any more. Instead she offers supper and cards. It's a charity to accept, so you should. But don't play with his lordship, my dear. He will fleece you unmercifully. I'm afraid he uses these evenings as an opportunity to pay his bills."

The day before the event, the Earl came into the drawing room with a note in his hand.

"I'm afraid I have to go to Overshott immediately. Something has come up I need to deal with personally. We'll have to miss the Barnstable supper, I'm afraid. I'll send a note."

Louise had been looking forward to playing cards again and was incensed her husband should automatically assume she would not go without him.

"No," she replied. "I wish to go. I shall stay here. I shall write to present your excuses and go alone. It would be churlish for both of us to stay away. Lady Barnstable might think we are avoiding her because of her circumstances. Your grandmother told me about it all."

"If you wish," said her husband, irritated that his wife should be as happy without his company as with it, "but it will be an insipid evening, and stay away from the host. He'll take your last sixpence if you give him the chance."

Louise arrived by herself at the Barnstables' rather shoddy townhouse. It was her first outing alone as the Countess and though she felt a twinge of anxiety at not having her husband's reassuring bulk by her side, on the whole she was happy to be free. She no longer had to appear the perfect wife.

By now she knew most of the people at the soirée and was greeted in a friendly manner, though naturally most people asked after her husband.

Hearing this, their host, called out jovially, "When the cat's away, the mice will play, eh, my lady?" and though she hadn't really taken to the man and felt sorry for his wife, she had to admit he had just about hit the nail on the head. She gave him a brief smile.

Supper passed pleasantly enough. The fare was very simple: a thin soup followed by a dish of ham with leeks. It was tasty but rather salty. She did not know that Lord Barnstable always instructed his cook to over-season the meal when they had guests for cards. It made people drink rather more of his inferior wine. And those who drank tended to make mistakes. He watched the new Countess of Shrewsbury and was disappointed when she took no wine.

No port was offered for the gentlemen at the end of the simple meal and when they rose from table Lord Barnstable quickly took Louise by the arm. He had heard she was an inexperienced card player. Her husband was one of the wealthiest men in London. And he wasn't there to keep an eye on her. Perfect.

"Come, my dear," he said. "Be my partner in a rubber of whist. I'll stake us against any others here."

He said this last part loud, and immediately had takers. Many saw it as an opportunity to win back some of their losses, for though Barnstable was a formidable player, they thought Lady Shrewsbury a novice.

In the end, she and Shrewsbury were partnered with Lord and Lady Veness. They played a few rubbers, and Louise was careful to appear neither too clever nor too obviously inexperienced. They ended up losing narrowly.

"I fancy you played better when I partnered you," said Lord Veness.

"Yes, you were so kind," replied Louise. "Lord Barnstable's swift play frightens me a little."

As intended, her response pleased both gentlemen, Veness because he interpreted it to mean she thought him the greater gentleman, and her host because it confirmed his sense of superiority.

"Come, come," he said. "You'll have people thinking I'm an ogre. Play a hand of piquet against me and I'll show you how it's done. Lord and Lady Veness will excuse us, I'm sure."

By now Louise was thoroughly sick of her host's condescending attitude and was keen to show *him* how it was done. Their partners bowed their acquiescence, and she and Barnstable moved to a table off to one side.

"Allow me to bring you a glass of wine, my dear," he said. "I need one and I'm sure you do too."

"Oh, yes please," she said, for she was thirsty. "At least, not wine, if you please. I don't drink it. A glass of lemonade would be wonderful."

"Certainly." He bowed and left her.

She looked around and saw only one footman bringing refreshment to the guests. Supper had been served by this one footman and the butler. They obviously couldn't afford more staff.

It was a point in his favor that Lord Barnstable did not disdain to serve himself and her.

Her host returned a few minutes later with a glass of wine in one hand, but in the other something that certainly was not lemonade.

"I'm sorry, Lady Shrewsbury, we seem to have run out of lemons. I hope you will not despise this glass of orgeat I made for you. My wife likes the flavor of almonds."

"I'm sure it will be delicious." Louise received the glass and took a long swallow. She really was very thirsty.

Lord Barnstable watched with satisfaction. In fact, he had poured a measure of whiskey into the bottom of the glass, counting on the nutty flavor of the orgeat to conceal its presence.

Louise found the drink peculiar but not really unpleasant. At least it quenched her thirst.

Play began and she quickly saw her opponent really was a fine player. In spite of a fleeting sensation that the pips on the cards were swimming before her eyes, she concentrated hard and won enough to keep him on his mettle. At the end of the first *partie* they were about even. Barnstable challenged her again.

"Let us increase the stakes, my dear," he said. "I see you have been hiding your light under a bushel. You are a formidable opponent. It's a pity to waste your talent on a few pence.

They set the wager at ten shillings a point. This time Louise deliberately went down to the tune of twenty pounds, a sum she could easily afford. She wanted him to underestimate her and it was she who challenged him to a third round. She was determined, in spite of the odd disembodied feeling that had grown on her during the last game, to put him in his place.

"I shall not let you beat me again," she said. "It must not be thought a lady cannot beat a gentleman."

"In that case, let us increase the stakes," he suggested with a smile. "If you are to beat me, let it be for something worth winning.

What do you say to a pound a point and an extra hundred on the whole?"

This was heavy betting, but she was sure she could beat him. Besides, if she lost, she could afford it. Since Gareth had paid all her dress bills, she was financially well in hand. She still had five hundred pounds of her allowance. That would be more than enough! And she wanted to put her husband in his place, too. He had warned her off playing with the host. How delightful it would be to announce large winnings. That would show him she wasn't just a complaisant little wife!

"Very well, my lord," she said.

"But before we play, let me fetch you another glass of orgeat," offered her host. That is, unless you found it disagreeable?"

"No, indeed. Thank you, that would be kind. I am very thirsty."

Barnstable smiled and disappeared. He came back with another glass of wine for himself and a larger glass of the same drink as before for Louise. She drank deeply and the cards were dealt.

Louise began by winning on points, but the feeling of oddness increased, as if it were not she who was playing but someone else. She drained the rest of the orgeat in her glass and they began the second hand. Now the cards swam before her eyes and she found she was unable to concentrate. She was increasingly sleepy. It was not surprising, she said to herself, trying to talk herself awake. She had not been sleeping well and she had never before played against so cunning an opponent. She lost that hand, but by how much, she did not know. Her opponent looked at her narrowly as she inexpertly dealt the third and last hand. He continued to play with a precision she found she could not match. She could hardly keep her eyes open. All she wanted to do was lie down. She kept him at bay for a while but then made one silly mistake after another and ended up losing badly.

When Lord Barnstable announced her final losses, the shock made her sit up. Over seven hundred pounds, an enormous sum! Much more than she had.

"Can it possibly be as much as that?" she gulped. "I had no idea! But... I haven't the means to pay it."

She waited but he said nothing to relieve her, so she continued hesitatingly, "I... I must ask you, dear Lord Barnstable, to take my vowels. I will not be able to pay you in full till quarter day."

"Dear lady," he said gently, "You put me in a difficult position. You say you have not the sum to pay what you owe. That is indeed a misfortune for any person of honor. One does not wager without being able to cover the loss. Debts of honor, you know must be paid at once."

Louise's head was aching now and she was beginning to feel sick. All she could think of was getting out of that stuffy room into the fresh air. What could she do? She could offer to pay what she had and ask him to wait for the rest. But he had just indicated he would not extend her credit. She rushed into a foolish decision.

"Would you... would you take this as an earnest of future payment?"

And she held out the Shrewsbury diamond bracelet.

Louise and Barnstable had been playing off to one side, and after the first hands, any onlookers had wandered off. She spoke quietly and no one else heard her. But the flash of the diamonds as she took the bracelet of her arm and handed it to Barnstable caught more than one eye, and the murmur *family jewel* ran around the room.

Lord Barnstable looked at her seriously, saying nothing. *Let her sweat,* he thought. But his mind was working furiously. Her I.O.U was worth 700 pounds. That was a tidy sum, and one he would have been glad to collect. If the silly wench didn't have it, her husband did. But the bracelet was worth much more, not because he could sell it, but because he knew Shrewsbury would pay anything to get it back.

Finally he spoke. "Very well, my dear. As your, er, well-wisher, let us not talk of vowels and debts but rather of an arrangement between friends. I will, er, *hold* the bracelet for now."

And who knows what else you might be prepared to pay, said his ever-active voice in his head.

Louise looked at him, her head swimming.

"Thank you, my lord," she said. "That is very kind of you. Now I must… must…."

She ran from the room and down the stairs. Without stopping for her cloak, she wrenched open the front door and took a gulp of the cool night air. She ran down the linkway to where her coach was waiting and leaped inside, but they were hardly underway before she had to call to him desperately to stop. She flung herself from the carriage and was violently sick into the bushes that grew along the edge of the park in the center of the square.

Chapter Forty-Five

Rose had been enjoying life immensely. She was senior to Susan and treated with respect in the household. She sat at table just under the butler and housekeeper, on a level with his lordship's valet.

Her duties had become heavier, it was true, and she was glad to share them. Her ladyship's fine gowns took a good deal more looking after than her old clothes, and more expertise with the needle was required for the inevitable damage to the hems. Luckily, Susan had learned a lot from her Aunt Booth and could take over the repairs. It was she who cleaned the maligned wedding gown and hung it up in the room she now shared with Rose. Rose took over the duties of tea tray, hot water, and general putting away of her ladyship's things, and they divided up the dressing and undressing. The one other thing Susan did consistently and successfully was her ladyship's hair.

For Rose, a pleasant side effect of having a co-worker was that she could spend more time at the kitchen door with Freddy. After seeing her in the street with her mistress that day, it had not taken him long to discover her whereabouts. They were now walking out regularly, and on Rose's days off he took her to all sorts of sights: Madame Tussauds, Astley's Equestrian Review, and her favorite, the Vauxhall Gardens.

They couldn't stay there late; it was a long journey back across the river and she had to be home by midnight, but she was charmed when all the lanterns in the trees were turned on at once. It was like magic! Freddy treated her to a supper of the famous shaved ham and a glass of wine. She was entirely unaccustomed to alcohol of any sort, and it went straight to her head. She let Freddy kiss her in the boat on the way home, but he was a perfect gentleman and didn't press her for more.

It wasn't long after The Kiss (as it figured in her mind) that Freddy began talking about their future.

"I'm beginnin' to fink it might be time for me to settle down," he said, "if I can just get a bit put aside. I'm doin' all right, but a wife costs. I wouldn't want 'er to 'ave to work."

"A wife?" Rose couldn't believe her ears. Did he mean her? They'd only been going together for a month.

"You got someone in mind?" she asked timidly.

"Yes, and you knows who it is, Miss Rose Brady! I 'opes you don't go kissin' just anyone!"

"No I don't, and you know it! But you 'aven't even met me Ma and Da."

"No, and I ain't goin' to until I've got enough by me to prove I can keep a wife."

Rose was struck by the justice of this. Her father certainly wouldn't let her marry someone who couldn't support her. She was the youngest in the family, and the prettiest. She'd always been his favorite.

"I just needs another bit 'o luck," continued Freddy, "like sellin' that story to me mate at the newspaper. You ain't got a juicy bit o' gossip for me, ave yer?"

"No. M'lady was a bit put out the other day and I thought she might be, you know, increasing, but she 'asn't said nothin'."

"She had a bit of a barney wiv me lord?"

"No, nothin' like that. I've never 'eard any arguments. We don't see a lot of 'im to tell the truth. 'E's always in the 'Ouse o' Lords.

Afternoons we does our walk, then she does 'er funny drawins and they goes out most nights."

"Funny drawins?" Freddy pricked up his ears.

"Yes. She's ever so good at them. People she meets, she makes pictures of them lookin' well, funny. Carrycat-yours, or something, she calls 'em."

"You got any of 'em? I'd like ter 'ave a look, if they're funny like you say. I can always do wiv a laugh."

"No, but I specks I can borrow 'em and show you."

"'Ow about termorrer?"

"It's not my day off!"

"I know that, yer silly. I'll just come by and you can let me 'ave 'em. I'll bring 'em back when I takes yer out next week. Tell yer what, we'll 'ave pie and peas down on the river. We'll get an 'ackney and spend the day. I'll take yer for a row. Y'can wear a pretty bonnet, and I'll wear a proper 'at instead of me cap, like the toffs."

The vision of herself floating along in her new bonnet filled Rose with delight. It didn't occur to her to wonder why Freddy was so keen to see a pile of funny pictures that he couldn't wait till next week, but she didn't think her mistress would mind. She always said they were just for fun.

Rose was late to bed after her day off and was still sleeping when Susan went to help their mistress get ready. The Countess was going to breakfast with the Dowager and was leaving the house early. So she missed the opportunity to ask her about the funny pictures and in fact had forgotten all about it when Freddy showed up at the back door.

"Sorry I can't stop," he said. "I got a lot of deliv'ries today and I need to get on. Where's them carrycat-yours, then?"

"Oh! I forgot!" exclaimed Rose. "And now she's gone, so I can't ask 'er."

"But she won't mind, shorely. Y'said yerself it's only a bunch o' funny pictures."

"Yes, that's what she always says." Rose made up her mind. "Oh, all right, then. I'll run and get them."

Rose ran upstairs and took the portfolio of caricatures from the desk drawer where she knew her mistress kept it. She extracted the top ten or so pages with the most recent images and put them between the pages of the previous day's newspaper she'd taken from the kitchen table. She didn't want them to get dirty. She went back downstairs and gave them to Freddy.

"Don't lose 'em, will you?" she said. "Make sure you bring 'em back when I sees yer next week, on me day off, as usual. Don't forget!"

"I won't," he said, running up the steps to the street and giving her a cheery wave.

It wasn't until he was well away from Grosvenor Square that he dropped into one of the small parks, sat on a bench and opened the newspaper.

His eyes opened wide and a grin split his face. Here it was. This was going to make him a pile, or his name wasn't Frederick Musgrove. He'd begun to think the money he was spending on Rose was going to prove a waste, but this 'ere was a bit of all right.

Chapter Forty-Six

Louise felt a little better after vomiting, but when she at last got into her bed she found her head spun every time she closed her eyes. She finally managed to sleep, but awoke with a sore, dry throat and an aching head. She couldn't imagine what had made her so unwell. Could something at the Barnstables' supper have been bad?

Then the awful truth of what she had done flooded through her. She had offered the Shrewsbury bracelet to cover a debt! What could she have been thinking? All she could remember was feeling desperate to get away from there. She would get the bracelet back when she paid the debt, but it wasn't hers to give away, even for a day! It belonged to her husband's family! It was nothing less than theft! Her husband must never find out!

It wasn't until she had gulped down two cups of the scalding hot tea Susan brought that her fevered brain was able to form a plan. She would write to the kindly Arnold Booking, her husband's man of business. She would ask for an advance on her allowance and have it delivered to Barnstable. No! She could not write that in a note, someone might see it! She would ask Booking to wait on her this afternoon and have him send a draft to Barnstable. She wouldn't mention the bracelet. Just have him think it was a normal gambling debt. He'd be shocked, of course, but he was the soul of discretion. Barnstable would return the bracelet and Gareth would never notice it was missing. Yes! That was the solution!

She scribbled the note to Mr. Booking and told Susan to deliver it personally. The fewer people who knew about it the better. She still felt poorly and would have put off her breakfast meeting with the Dowager if she could. But she knew they were to lunch with one of her ladyship's friends and it would be very rude to cancel at such short notice.

She ate nearly nothing of the delicious breakfast put before her at the Dowager's, but since her hostess herself ate like a bird, she did not find it remarkable. When they visited the chic establishments where her ladyship bought her delicious headwear, Louise tried to appear her normal self and laughed off the fact she dared buy nothing.

"I'm sorry," she said, "but I have to draw in the bustle a bit this quarter. You've no idea how high my bill at Véronique's is!"

"Tush!" said her grandmama-in-law, "Gareth is rich enough to buy an abbey. Send him the bills!"

"Oh," said Louise. "I don't feel comfortable doing that. He makes me a very generous allowance, you know."

Then she felt like crying when she considered that was true, and she had repaid him by wagering away the family bracelet.

The old friend of Lady Esmé's they were lunching with had been intimate with a very dashing group in her youth. At table she recounted scurrilous stories about people who were now either dead or in their dotage. It was odd to hear the two old ladies, both now the model of propriety, talk of the scandalous behavior of their contemporaries fifty years before. But it had the effect of cheering Louise up. Somehow it made her own transgression seem almost forgivable. It's not as if she'd given the bracelet to a lover, or worn it as her only item of clothing when dancing on the table!

But when she returned home, a note was waiting for her with Mr. Booking's apologies. Due to other business, he could not oblige her that afternoon, but would do himself the honor of waiting on her the next day, if she was free. This was a blow. She had hoped to settle the affair before the Earl returned. He was expected for dinner. But no matter, instead of having Booking come to her, as soon as her husband left for the House in the morning she would go to him. Having missed a couple of days, Gareth was bound to go to his boxing session. She could slip out of the house and be back before he returned.

The Earl came back from Overshott that evening in a good humor. Whatever his business had been, it appeared to have prospered. Unusually, they were not invited anywhere and dined together at home. Over dinner he asked Louise with a smile what she'd been doing while he was away. In fact, he'd missed her and had returned determined to get to the bottom of whatever it was that had made her so difficult recently.

"How did you fare at the Barnstable card party?" he asked pleasantly.

Louise started. She had hoped to avoid the subject altogether.

"Oh, I, er, it was quite entertaining," she said shortly.

"Whom did you partner?"

"I played against Mr. Veness with Lord Barnstable." That was at least part of the truth.

Gareth laughed. "A sheep and a wolf!"

"Both gentlemen were… were very… kind." She desperately wanted the conversation to end.

"Barnstable? Kind? I find that hard to believe!" Her husband looked at her narrowly. Why was she so uncomfortable?

"Believe what you like, my lord. Now I'll say goodnight. I have a headache."

Louise went straight up to her apartment. She couldn't believe what she had said. It wasn't true she had a headache; that had cleared up, thankfully. But she had not slept well the night before and the day had been fraught with worry about the bracelet. Overwhelmed, she lay on her bed and wept.

Her husband was astonished at her response. She had never been openly hostile before. He shook his head, sighed and took himself off to his club. He noticed a hush in the conversation as he came into the card room, but thought nothing of it. In the corner, his friend Tommy Ainsworth was playing piquet with Rupert Brown, a gentleman recently returned from India and whom Gareth knew only slightly. He liked playing with Ainsworth himself, and went over and sat following the game until the *partie* ended.

Then Rupert Brown said, "You missed an interesting game of piquet last night at Barnstable's, Shrewsbury."

"No need to bring that up, Brown," said Ainsworth, "There's no proof of any of it."

The Earl's interest was well engaged by this time. "Well, what did I miss?"

"Your wife lost an important piece of jewelry to Barnstable. The Shrewsbury diamond bracelet. And ran from the room in tears. At least, that's what they're saying."

"Is this true, Tommy?" The Earl turned to his friend, a fierce frown on his face.

"Look, Gary, I didn't see anything. The rumor is going around that Lady Shrewsbury gave Barnstable her bracelet. But as I say, I didn't see it and it's probably all just gossip."

"Barnstable was looking mighty pleased with himself, that's all I can say," interposed Rupert Brown. "And she'd been his only partner all evening. Until she ran away."

"Look, Gary." His friend gripped him on the shoulder. "Best you ask her. It's probably all a mistake. Perhaps he was just fixing the clasp or something."

"But she wasn't wearing it when she left, that I do know," persisted Rupert. "I looked particularly."

"If the clasp was tricky, she could have put it in her reticule. And she probably realized it was er... late and left in a hurry." Tommy seemed determined to find an innocent explanation. "As I said, why don't you just ask her."

"I shall. If the clasp is loose," said the Earl calmly, "we need to get it fixed. Now, Ainsworth, if you've lost enough to Brown here, how about losing to me?" He desperately wanted to get home to his wife, but wouldn't let it show. He leaned forward and picked up the cards.

Chapter Forty-Seven

Louise had been in bed for some time but was still trying to sleep when her husband's characteristic short knock sounded at the communicating door. Before she could think of a way to say she was indisposed and couldn't receive him, he was at her side.

She sat up, her heart beating suddenly against her ribs. "M... my lord!" she stammered.

"My lady!" he responded. All the earlier good humor had disappeared from his face.

He stalked up and down once or twice before standing in front of her and saying abruptly, "Disturbing intelligence concerning you reached my ears in the club this evening. I cannot believe it to be true, but it would settle my mind to have you deny it."

In vain did she try to answer lightly. Her words caught in her throat and all she could stammer was, "D... deny what?"

"That you gave the Shrewsbury bracelet to Barnstable in payment of a gambling debt."

"Wh... who told you?"

"You don't deny it, then?"

"I... I...."

There were no words to explain her action, which now seemed unbelievable. Even if she could have found them, she was incapable of saying anything coherent. Her throat had closed shut and not a sound would come out. Tears came to her eyes, and though she tried to wipe them away on her bedsheet, they came faster than she could control.

"Very affecting," sneered her husband. "But I require an answer. Did you or did you not give the bracelet to Barnstable in payment of a gambling debt?"

"Yes... no... yes, that is...." She wanted to say she hadn't given it away. But she couldn't explain it was simply being held until she could pay her debt.

"Yes or no? Answer me plainly."

She collapsed entirely, her body wracked with sobs. "Yes. Bu... but I was unwell. My head was aching and I just wanted to get away. I... I was vilely sick afterwards...."

But her husband didn't seem to have heard. "And may I ask what the sum was for which you sold a piece of property that has been in my family for three generations?"

"S...seven h...hundred p...pounds."

The words came out as shuddering sobs. Why couldn't she say she hadn't *sold* it? But it was no use.

The Earl looked at her for a long moment then turned on his heel and left. Louise clutched the sheet to her face and sobbed and sobbed. She wept because she was stupid, she wept because she had done something unforgivable, she wept because she had irretrievably lost the only man she would ever love.

She finally wept herself into a fitful sleep from which she awoke to cry again. Thus she passed the worst night of her life, crying and waking, waking and crying. When Rose brought in her tea she was shocked by her ladyship's appearance.

"Oh, m'lady, you do look ever so bad. Shall I ask Mr. Lisle to call the doctor?"

"No, I have the headache, that's all. The tea will revive me, thank you."

And Rose went away, thinking again that her ladyship must be increasing. That would explain her moody ups and downs. She was never like that normally.

Chapter Forty-Eight

The Earl returned to his room furious with his wife, furious with himself for not forbidding her to go to the card party, and furious with Lord Barnstable. He must have seen she was a novice! How in the name of God had he persuaded her to play for such high stakes she'd wagered the bracelet? One thing for sure, he would have it out with Barnstable and get the bracelet back, no matter what it cost.

He, too, slept poorly and the following morning went to Jackson's boxing saloon. He attacked the man the trainer put up against him with such ferocity Gentleman Jim stopped the bout after two rounds.

"If yer wanting to kill someone, me lord," he said, "you've come to the wrong place. Now go and take it out on the sawdust bag and then have a good cold hose down. Don't come back 'ere till you've cooled off. I mean it! If you was the Prince Regent 'imself, I wouldn't 'ave none of that behavior from yer."

Knowing he was in the wrong made Gareth even more angry, but he did as he was told. He punched the sawdust bag until sweat was running down his body and his knuckles were sore. He submitted to the cold hose, forcing himself to stand under it till his teeth were chattering. Then he went home and furiously downed a copious breakfast without tasting a bite. At about eleven he presented himself at the Barnstables' shoddy residence.

The old butler who answered the door was surprised to see him so early in the morning and answered his demand to see Lord Barnstable doubtfully.

"His lordship is generally not abroad so early, my lord. But if you would be so kind as to wait in the library, I shall inquire."

"Do so, but tell him the longer I wait the less I shall have to offer. That should bring him down pretty smartly."

The old man shook his head in puzzlement, but dutifully conveyed the message.

It was therefore not more than fifteen minutes later that a rosy-faced Lord Barnstable, still bearing evidence of a hasty shave, came bustling into the library.

"Shrewsbury!" he said cordially, holding out his hand. "What an unexpected pleasure!"

"I hardly think so," responded his visitor coldly, refusing to take the hand. "You must have been in hourly expectation of seeing me."

"Well, since you put it so bluntly, I did think you would turn up sooner or later. But I was told you was at Overshott. All's well there, I hope?" Barnstable tried to inject a note of bonhomie into the conversation.

"Whatever may or may not be happening at Overshott is none of your concern. What *is* however your concern, and mine, is the return of my property."

"Ah! Yes, I see. You are a man who likes to come quickly to the point. I, too, prefer the direct approach, but may I offer you a glass of something before we talk terms?"

"No and we will talk no terms."

Then the offer of a drink jogged the memory of something his wife had said. She had been ill. Her head ached. She had been sick. He looked at Lord Barnstable with scorn written clearly all over his face.

"And from what my wife tells me, I'm sure you offered her something to drink too. Something that would enable you to take advantage of her."

Barnstable blustered, "I say, old man... that's... that...."

"That's the truth and you know it. I've always known you for a fool, Barnstable, but I've never known you for a cad. Now do as I say and I won't tell everyone in the clubs that you deliberately inebriated my wife because you were in danger of losing to her. You will tell anyone who asks that Lady Shrewsbury asked you to look at the clasp of her bracelet. You determined it was broken and recommended she not wear it any more. She put it in her reticule. Is that understood?"

"My dear fellow...."

"Don't *dear fellow* me. Is that understood?"

Barnstable nodded.

"Good. Now, my wife tells me she gave you the Shrewsbury bracelet to pay a debt of seven hundred pounds. I will give you precisely that sum here, now, today."

"Well, now, Shrewsbury," Barnstable tried to regain control of the situation. "There is the little matter of interest and...."

Before he could say another word, his visitor clutched him fiercely by the throat and forced him back against the library door.

Barnstable tried to pull those strong hands away, but the grip around his throat tightened inexorably until the perimeter of his vision began to fade.

"Perhaps you misheard me," said Lord Shrewsbury calmly. "I said I would pay you exactly what my wife says she owed you. I also told you not to waste my time. The sum will decrease by fifty pounds for every minute you keep me waiting. I advise you to hurry up."

"Yes, yes," croaked Barnstable. The grip on his throat slackened. "Seven hundred pounds. Very well."

"You're lucky. If it were anything but a debt of honor you may be sure I would see you in hell before I paid a penny of it. And there's still the matter of your abusing my wife. You may be sure I won't forget it. The next time you invite us to one of your paltry little evenings, we will come. She will play with you and you will make sure she wins. Not that I doubt she could win on her own merits when she's not been deliberately inebriated by her host. You, sir, are no gentleman."

The Earl let go of his adversary, who staggered back and sat down, his hands at his throat. Gareth put his hand inside his coat and removed his pocketbook. From it he extracted seven one hundred pound notes.

"Get the bracelet. Hurry. I may change my mind."

"You devil," rasped Barnstable.

He could not run, but he staggered as fast as he could to the door and reappeared not more than five minutes later.

"Here, take the damned thing."

He thrust the bracelet at the Earl who took it, put it in his pocket and handed him the banknotes.

Barnstable had sat down again and was gingerly feeling his throat.

"You nearly throttled me, you swine!" He swallowed painfully.

"Yes, and if I hear you've mentioned this affair to anyone, I'll come back and finish the job. Remember, you will say you offered to look at the clasp on the bracelet, and she put it in her reticule. That's why she wasn't wearing it when she left this god-forsaken pile the other night. No one but a cad would have engaged a naïve woman to play for such high stakes and then slipped something into her drink. Consider yourself lucky I feel honor bound to settle her debt and don't broadcast that information."

"She's not as naive as you think, Shrewsbury," croaked Barnstable as the Earl left the library. "She played a pretty deep game, and it's my belief she's playing you too. I hope she wins."

Chapter Forty-Nine

Louise was still in bed when her husband returned. After drinking her tea she had fallen into an exhausted sleep from which he roused her saying her name loudly but not fondly. She woke with a start and looked up into his unsmiling face.

"Here," he said, tossing the bracelet onto the embroidered coverlet. "We're engaged at the Westovers' tonight. You will wear it, and continue to wear it often. There should be no need for any explanation but if necessary, you will say the clasp was loose. You handed it to Barnstable to see if he could tighten it. He could not, so you put it in your reticule."

He paused, then continued. "I do you the credit of believing that had Barnstable not deliberately made you drunk, you would not have acted as you did. You are too trusting, Louise. You think yourself awake on all counts, but you are not. Women may have more qualities than society gives them credit for, but you still need a man to protect you."

Without waiting for a response, he turned and left her.

Drunk? Louise looked at his departing back with astonishment. Barnstable had made her drunk? Of course! She had started feeling peculiar after he brought her that first glass. And she had drunk that even bigger glass after the second hand! What a fool she was! Gareth was right. She looked at the bracelet with loathing. She never wanted to wear it again. She had forgotten about the

Westovers and longed to send regrets, but the tone in her husband's voice didn't admit of any refusal.

Her demeanor at the party that night would never have led anyone to believe that every moment was torture to her. She willingly joined in the silly games the hostess had arranged for her guests' amusement. The bracelet sparkled on her arm and though more than one person nudged another with a look of enquiry, nothing was said about it. The Earl was as attentive to his wife as a newlywed might be expected to be, and while they would hardly have been described as love's young dream, they both seemed perfectly happy.

The next two weeks continued in the same way. At home the couple was rarely together and their discourse was polite but distant. In the evenings at their friends' they were always together, her ladyship cool and elegant, the Earl no more than his usual scowling self.

The only person who noticed anything amiss was the Dowager. She began arriving without invitation just before lunch or tea and would crumble a tiny portion of whatever was being served, pretending to eat, while narrowly observing the newlyweds.

"It was a good idea to take your meals in here," she observed one day at lunch. "The view over the garden is delightful. It's a pity the weather has been so changeable. I've never seen so much rain at this time of the year."

Louise looked at the garden and shuddered visibly. She was glad it was too wet to sit outside. She hated the garden now and never went out there.

"I shall be glad to get to Overshott," said the Earl. "I wonder how the wheat is doing. It'll be no good if it's waterlogged. But I think perhaps Louise will stay here. There can be nothing to do in the country if it's too wet to go outside."

Louise looked at him in surprise. This was the first she had heard of staying in London without him. The Dowager had caught her shudder at the mention of the garden and now saw the look. She had heard about the bracelet, of course. The network of women's intelligence was better than a newspaper. But as far as she knew the rumor had been proven false. Now she wondered what the truth of the matter was. She was sorry, for she genuinely liked Louise and thought her a good wife for her difficult grandson.

Before she left she therefore said in an off-hand way, "Oh, by the way, Gareth, I need you to come and see me tomorrow some time. It doesn't matter when. I have some papers I'd like your advice about."

"Papers? What papers? I know nothing about it."

"Do you imagine you know everything about my private business? My dear boy, a woman must have some secrets. But we can't talk about it now. We need the thing in front of us."

"Have you a secret lover, Gran, who's threatening to expose you? Is that it?"

"Certainly not, and if I had, I shouldn't keep it a secret. I'd be proud of it!"

The Earl kissed his grandmother's cheek lovingly. "I expect you would! And I should have to pay him off to prevent him publishing scandalous stories about you in the papers."

She tapped him on the chest with her fan. "Yes. And then forgive me without recrimination. That is another of the responsibilities of being the head of the family."

He looked at her closely. "I'll see you tomorrow," he said.

Chapter Fifty

"So where are those papers, then, Gran?" said the Earl, coming into her elegant bedroom at nine the following morning. He had important business in the House later on, so had breakfasted quickly and early and was there by nine. He knew she was awake by that hour, though she usually didn't rise until later.

"Good morning, Gareth," she replied pointedly. "Don't you know not to visit ladies so early? We need a chance to prepare ourselves."

Since his grandmother was wearing a very becoming nightcap with a jaunty bow by her ear and a lovely peignoir with deep lace trim, his lordship was not fooled.

"Nonsense! You are obviously entertaining that lover we were talking about yesterday. Where is he? Hiding under the bed? Should I have brought a sword to run him through?"

Lady Esmé trilled a laugh. "Silly boy! And you know there are no papers either. And if you call me Gran one more time I'll have a fit and die. Then you'll be sorry."

"No I won't. I should be rid of the most persistent thorn in my side." He kissed her cheek.

"Perhaps, though from what I hear, you have another thorn. And if I'm not mistaken, instead of dealing with it gently as Nanny would have done, you've ripped it from your side and left a gaping hole."

The Earl sighed and sat down on another of the spindly gold chairs he so disliked. "I collect I am to have a peal rung over me,

Grandmother, but for God's sake speak plainly. Enough of these riddles! What have I done, or not done, now?"

"Very well. I'm of the belief your wife wagered the Shrewsbury bracelet in a card game with Barnstable but you got it back. I will not ask how, though whatever you did to that cad he richly deserved. But instead of being happy with its return, you are treating your wife like a criminal. Why?"

"Damn it, Gran! Oh, excuse me! How you know these things beats me. You're right, of course. But you don't expect me to thank Louise for the opportunity to be of service to her, do you?"

"No, I expect you to forgive her, dry her tears of repentance, kiss her, and get about making that great-grandson I want to hold before I die."

"But she's been treating me like a stranger for weeks. Even before this whole fiasco she wouldn't let me kiss her or… the other thing."

"You mean she rejected you from the beginning, on your wedding night?"

"No!" The Earl thought for a moment, then decided to tell the truth. "That's just it! She seemed, well, keen. But then all of a sudden it was No!"

"What happened?"

"Damned (sorry! sorry!) if I know. She seemed vexed with me for some reason."

"Have you been seeing the Courtland woman?"

"No! She couldn't wait to replace me, and I broke with her. She was getting on my nerves anyway."

"So when did Louise start saying no?"

"After the Ball."

"Didn't you ask her why?"

"Of course not! I'm not going to argue with a woman who makes it clear she doesn't want me."

"Hmm. That's odd. Just before the Ball began, she said *I promise I will always do my best for the family and the Earl.* That was when she was proudly showing me and her mother the lanterns in the garden. But yesterday when I mentioned the garden she shuddered visibly. Is it possible something happened there to make her angry? Angry enough to reject you and lose the Shrewsbury bracelet in a wager?"

"Nothing happened anywhere at the Ball! It was a great success. You said so yourself!"

"But Diane Courtland was there. I suppose she prevailed on that silly little Youngbrough to take her. God knows I didn't invite her. Did Louise see you alone together?"

"No! We were never alone together!"

But as he said it, he remembered. They had been alone together. The meeting in the garden! Could Louise have seen them there? Then he recalled her red eyes and the story about her walking into a tree branch. Was that it? Did she see them and somehow get the wrong impression? But how? All he did was tell Diane it was over.

"Damn it all! Why today of all days?" he exploded. "There's the last reading of a Bill I sponsored and the vote will be close. I can't miss it. I don't have time now to go home and have it out with her."

"You will not go home at any time and *have it out with her!*" cried his grandmother. "Just listen to yourself! This is your wife we are talking about. The future mother of your children, God willing. You will go home after whatever nonsense it is you have going on in the House, take her by the hand, explain the mistake and beg her forgiveness. You will not scowl and frighten her."

"She's not frightened by my scowls."

"Then even more reason to make love to her. She must be the only woman in London who isn't. I tell you, Gareth, I like Louise. I've liked her from the start. Trust you to make such a mull of it."

"*I? I* make a mull of it?!" The Earl was incensed. "She gives away an irreplaceable piece of family jewelry and *I* made a mull of it?"

"Yes. Just like a man. But she'll forgive you if you ask her nicely." His grandmother smiled at him sweetly. "Aren't you late for your vote in the House? Off you go. You may kiss me."

And she proffered her downy cheek.

Chapter Fifty-One

Louise had spent most of the morning in her rooms, eaten a solitary lunch and then rang for Rose to come with her for a walk. Their afternoon perambulations had recently been interrupted by the rainy weather but today it was dry. Louise felt she would go mad if she didn't get out of the house.

She was still trying to come to terms with her husband's announcement the previous day that she would be staying in the capital while he went to Overshott. The thought appalled her. To be away from him for as much as three months! Oh! She had tried to tell herself she didn't care, that Diane was welcome to him, but she knew it wasn't true. Even after everything that had happened, after his cold words to her and hers to him, she loved him. She loved being next to him, putting her hand on his arm, feeling his hand under her elbow, sensing his solid form beside her. He had said women needed protection, and as much as she wanted to believe otherwise, she thought he was right. She couldn't be away from him for three months!

Rose came in now, and Louise was shocked how pale she had become. She had been so tied up with her own misery she hadn't realized she was seeing much more of Susan than of Rose.

"Rose, my dear," she said, sounding to her own ears like her mother, "whatever is the matter? Are you ill? Is something bothering you?"

Rose just shook her head mutely.

"Please tell me if there's something wrong. I should like to help you if I can."

Rose seemed on the point of saying something, but then shook her head again.

"No, m'lady," she said. "It's just all this rain. I 'ate bein' cooped up inside. It's much worse 'ere than at 'ome. I'll feel better for a walk."

And it did seem as if this were so. They walked down the now familiar streets and both smiled behind their gloves at the sight of the stout gentleman who had been unable to mount his horse before. This time he was chasing his hat down the street. It was an enormously tall effort, and a sudden buffet of wind blew it clean off his head. They never saw if he recovered it, as it was blown right across the road and down a side street, with the gentleman in hot pursuit.

But Rose was unusually quiet. She seemed lost in her own thoughts and only spoke when spoken to. When they got home, and the girl had disappeared downstairs for the tea, Louise rang for the housekeeper and asked her if she had noticed a problem with her.

"Yes, indeed," replied Mrs. Smith with a rueful smile. "I'm afraid she is unhappy in love."

"Oh!" This was something Louise could easily relate to and she nodded. "I see!"

"Yes. She was walking out regularly with a young man. A Freddy something. He was always at the kitchen door. I had to chase him away a couple of times. One of those cheeky, charming chaps all the maids go for. Then about two weeks ago he suddenly stopped coming. I know Rose waited a whole day for him in her best bonnet. She finally said something about having made a mistake, but we all knew he'd stood her up."

Louise remembered the young fellow who had raised his cap to them that day. "He's the one who delivers newspapers?"

"Yes, though how he got his job done with all the time he spent hanging around here, I don't know."

They were interrupted by the broad shape of the Earl, who appeared at the garden sitting room door. There was silence for a moment, and then Mrs. Smith, divining that he wanted to speak to his wife, curtseyed and left.

He came in and shut the door. "Louise," he said abruptly, "There's something I need to...," then, remembering his grandmother's admonitions, "No, goddam it! Look, Louise, I'm sorry."

She had risen and now came towards him.

"Sorry? What for?"

"For everything. For thinking that marriage was only..., that I could carry on... for Diane... for the bracelet...."

Louise made a choking sound and turned away.

"No! I mean, not for Diane, because I didn't... I mean, I hadn't seen her since we were married and in the garden she was trying to.... Dammit, Louise! I don't know what you think you saw but I didn't! Can you believe me?"

The effect of this incoherent speech was to make Louise turn around and fling herself against her husband's broad chest.

"Oh Gareth! Is it true? You haven't been...?" She turned her streaming eyes up at him.

"No, I haven't." Her husband regained his power of speech. "On my honor I haven't been with that woman since we were married. At the Ball, she insisted on seeing me in the garden and I told her it was all over. I should have told her before but I didn't. It was unfair to both of you. I'm sorry."

"Oh! How stupid I've been!"

Louise held her face against his waistcoat and cried. The Earl held her tight but said nothing. Finally, her sobbing ceased and she looked up at him again. She was not one of those women who could cry beautifully. Her plain face looked even worse than usual.

"Can you ever forgive me?" she hiccupped. "I've been so very, very foolish! I was angry and I wanted to make you pay. That's why... my expensive gowns... and refusing you. But not the bracelet! I didn't... I would never... Oh, I love you Gareth! That's why I did it all. I love you so much I couldn't think straight!"

Her husband didn't even notice how ugly she looked. At her words, he held her tighter and said with a laugh in his voice, "If loving me makes you give away the family jewels, order half a dozen of the most expensive gowns in the kingdom, and most of all, refuse to get rid of that damned contract, I'd definitely be better off if you didn't!"

She tried to smile. "I wanted to get rid of it, you don't know how much, Gareth! I've been so unhappy. I tried not to love you, but I couldn't!"

He looked down at her seriously. "You must know, Louise, when I married I didn't bargain for love. I just thought marriage was a necessary inconvenience. But if missing you when you're not there, and thinking about you when I should be thinking about something else, and wanting to punch the face of every man who puts his arm around you, my funny, clever, intensely irritating Louise Grey, I love you."

She threw her arms around his neck and kissed him.

"Upstairs," he said, when he could speak.

"What do you mean, upstairs?"

"You know very well what I mean."

"But what about the routine?"

"Damn the routine."

That night they missed dinner entirely and mortally offended the noble couple to whose Ball they had been invited but completely forgot to go.

Chapter Fifty-Two

The following morning the Countess slept late. Her morning tea remained untouched, her crumpled gown was in a heap from the previous evening, for her husband had told Lisle to allow no one upstairs unless they rang, and her petticoat and chemise were somewhere under the bed, when Rose burst into her bedchamber.

"Oh, m'lady, look! Look!" she cried. "I can't b'lieve he done it!"

"What? What?" Louise struggled from her sleep and sat up, realized she was naked and pulled the coverlet up to cover herself.

"Look!"

Taking the newspaper Rose was thrusting at her, she lay it flat upon the bed. There, looking back at her was the caricature of her husband she had done when they first met. It was grotesque but exactly like him, though now her fond eye regretted the scowl and the thin lips.

"What... how... who...?" she stammered

"It were Freddy, m'lady!" cried Rose, tears starting to her eyes, "'E said 'e just wanted to borrer them. But 'e never brought them back! On my life, I 'ad no idea what was in 'is mind!"

"You mean you gave my caricatures to this newspaper boy?"

"Yes!" the tears now fell in huge drops. "I didn't think you'd mind, m'lady! You always said they was just for fun. But now...."

Rose had at last understood that while the images, or most of them, were rather funny, the people depicted in them wouldn't think so. The tears ran unchecked down her cheeks. Louise, though she was still in something of a daze, noticed that, unlike her, her maid was one of those lucky women who could cry without disfiguring themselves. The tears glistened like gems on her long lashes and downy cheeks.

"I'm ever so sorry, m'lady," sobbed Rose, "I was right taken in by him. He said he wanted to marry me! But if I'd ever thought…."

Louise couldn't blame the girl. Just look what love had made *her* do!

"Don't cry, Rose," she said. "What you did was wrong, but you aren't the first to be taken in by a man. Why don't you go and make some tea for us both while I decide what to do."

Rose grabbed Louise's hand and kissed it. "Thank you, m'lady," she said and ran off. She had fully expected to be dismissed on the spot.

Louise quickly got out of bed and pulled on her nightgown. She retrieved her underclothes and gown from the floor and put them over a chair. Then she sat at her desk turning the pages of the newspaper. There they all were: Lady Wroxford with a nose like a needle, Lord Plimpton, his head reposing on what looked like a layered blancmange pudding, Mr. Pryce tripping on feet clad in baby booties, Mrs. Overton waving enormous hands in the manner of flippers, the honorable Beau Mainwaring's wife as a terrier on her hind legs, a ruff around her neck, a bow in her hair and her eyes shining as if she were expecting a bone and the gentleman with the lost hat spilling over the saddle of a horse that bowed visibly under his weight. But worst was the portrait of Diane Courtland. The others were perhaps unkind, but they were comic. That one was positively vitriolic.

Louise was hastily scanning the pages to see if the artist's name was anywhere mentioned. The editors had written:

> *We are pleased to present today a series of caricatures of some of the best known members of London society. The*

artist, who is clearly acquainted with them all and must be of their set, is known to us only as L S. What could the reason be for these cruelly comic depictions? We can only guess. A slight to be avenged? An enemy to be thwarted? A rival to be pilloried? We know not, but we hope to bring you more information as it becomes known to us.

She bit her lip, thinking furiously. There was no reason for anyone to associate her with the initials LS. Even if *Lady Shrewsbury* came up, who would believe she had done a caricature of her own husband? But would this Freddy give the name away? No, because he could be accused of theft. She was quite sure Rose would testify she had only loaned him the pictures. Pretty and naïve as she was, no one would disbelieve her.

At that point the girl herself returned with a tea tray and poured out a cup for her mistress.

"Have one yourself," said Louise. "You need it I as much as I do. Tell me, has his lordship seen this?"

"No 'e 'asn't. No one has, 'cept Mr. Lisle." Rose sniffed and wiped her nose on a screwed-up handkerchief. "It were late arrivin' this mornin'. He were ironing it an' I 'eard 'im shout out, like. You know 'im, 'e don't usually talk loud, so I went t'see what the problem was. He showed me. I said they was your friends and I thought you'd want t'see. So, bein' as 'is lordship is already gone to the 'Ouse, he give it t' me."

"Good. Put the newspaper in the library as usual and say nothing about it. Our best bet is to just act as if nothing is out of the ordinary. Try not to cry, though people will probably just think you're upset about Freddy. But apart from him, there's nothing to associate those pictures with us, and I don't think he'll show his face around here again."

"An' a good thing too!" said Rose fiercely. "I'd scratch 'is eyes out if I saw 'im." Then, after a pause, she continued, "If you please, m'lady, I've bin thinkin'. You 'ave all the reason in the world to dismiss me without a character. An' I deserve it. But if you can see your way clear, I'd like to go 'ome. I won't never talk about nothing, I promise. I thought I liked it 'ere, but I see now I was really only 'appy because of Freddy and 'e was a snake!" Tears came to her eyes again. "Please, m'lady, I miss me mum... and Jimmy."

"Jimmy?"

"Yes, we was walking out before I come to Lunnon. I was that stupid! I thought Freddy were a better catch, but I see now I was the one got caught. Jimmy would never serve me a trick like that."

She sniffed again and wiped her nose. "An' you've got Susan. She's better 'n me as a dresser, everybody knows that. If I can go back to Mrs. Grey, just as a parlor maid, that'd suit me."

"Are you sure? I'm not going to dismiss you to go because of... all this." Louise gestured at the newspaper. "We all make mistakes, especially where men are concerned. But if you truly want to go home, I can try to arrange it."

"Thank you, m'lady, thank you. I'll be better off there. I don't think I was made for bein' in a big city. I enjoyed all the sights, though. It'll be somethin' to tell my children." Rose seemed much more adult all of a sudden. "'Course, I'll have to tell Jimmy about what I done 'ere. But 'e loves me and I think 'e'll forgive me."

"If he really loves you, he will. And I wish you every happiness. I'll write to my mother and see if she'll take you back and then I'll ask his lordship if he'll spare a carriage to take you home."

"One with the picture on the sides?" Rose brightened visibly.

Louise laughed. "Yes, I think they've all got the coat of arms on the doors."

"Won't me mum be proud, seeing me drive up in that!"

Rose went off with a spring in her step to bring hot water for her ladyship.

Louise was fairly sure her mother would take Rose back because she was going to offer to pay her wage. She could afford it out of her allowance. And she was right. Mrs. Grey was pleased to have a pretty and biddable parlor maid. Her dresser, the formidable Wilkins, was surprised to see her niece back but never did know the truth of the matter. Rose kept to her story that she was homesick.

In fact, her employment in the Grey household was of short duration, for within a year she married her Jimmy and became mother to a number of children, all as pretty and amenable as herself. They were all very happy and never tired of their mother's stories about the Big City.

Chapter Fifty-Three

The Earl came home tired from a long sitting in the House, and after kissing his wife lovingly went up to change for dinner. It wasn't until they were at table that Louise introduced the topic of the caricatures.

"Did you see those extraordinary portraits in *The Times* today?" she said, feigning a nonchalance she didn't feel.

"What?" he answered, looking up from his plate which was claiming his full attention. Having missed dinner the night before, he had been unusually hungry all day.

"The caricatures in *The Times*?"

"Oh, them. Yes I saw them. Very funny, most of them."

"You weren't insulted by the one of you?"

He shrugged. "Why should I be?

"You don't wonder who LS might be? The person who drew them?"

"No. Who cares? I know I'm ugly. Doesn't take a caricature to tell me that."

"I don't think you're ugly."

He smiled at her. "You're blinded by post-coital affection, my dear. You'll come around."

"I am not! Anyway, by that measure you'll be saying I'm not ugly either, and we both know that's not true."

"I admit I didn't admire you when I met you, but it's been some weeks since I thought you plain. In fact, now I'm in a fair way of thinking you one of the handsomest women of my acquaintance."

He smiled at her again, and in his eyes was the deep, inscrutable look that had thrilled her before.

She smiled back lovingly. "Then you are suffering from the same sensation as I, my lord. Your senses are disordered."

The following morning, the Earl suggested they go to the bank and decide if she could bear to wear any of the other family jewels. The House had now sat down, and the summer recess had begun.

"Mind you," he said, giving her waist a squeeze, "I hesitate to offer, in case you decide to wager them all."

"How ungentlemanly to talk of that episode!" she protested, laughing. "No, I shall not do that ever again. Instead I shall leave vowels for enormous sums and you will be forced to pay them. And I shall order a gown embroidered with diamonds. I hear Princess Charlotte has bespoke such a one and I don't like to be outdone."

"It's a good thing we're going to Overshott next week, then. You won't find so many opportunities to ruin me."

She turned to him. "Really? Are we really both going? You're not leaving me behind?"

"No. I can't afford it." Then he looked rueful. "I'm sorry I said that the other day. It was unhandsome of me. I was angry. Of course you're coming with me. They are champing at the bit to see the new Countess. Besides, I should miss you... for other reasons."

He raised his eyebrows at her and she blushed.

They spent a pleasant hour at the bank examining the heavy old jewelry. The stones were good but the settings often ugly and of inferior metals. For some reason, gold was little used in the previous century.

"You know, I think we should have all these stones reset in gold," said Louise. "If you don't think it sacrilege to do so. Truly, no one is going to wear these, even if they have a short neck, like me. For one thing, it's so heavy! It would be like wearing a manacle. Feel it!"

The Earl hefted the necklace. "I see what you mean. Perhaps we should use it for a test like in the old days. Any woman wishing to marry the future Earl will have to wear the necklace solidly for a week without complaint. Only then will we know she's strong enough to bear the yoke."

They laughed together.

"But you're right," said the Earl. "Why don't we take the diamond necklace matching that infamous bracelet and you can sketch a possible new setting. Do you have any artistic talent? You told me once of all the womanly things you can't do, though I know one feminine talent you're very good at." He raised his eyebrows again. "But can you draw at all?"

Louise's heart gave a great lurch, and it was as much as she could do to make a suitable laughing response.

Chapter Fifty Four

The weather having finally settled down, they enjoyed a drive in the park that afternoon. Louise wore her new carriage dress of fine blue-grey wool with a fitted bodice and full skirt. It emphasized her slimness.

"Milady has the perfect figure for the present straight up and down mode," Véronique had said, frowning a little over the carriage dress. "But already I see the fashions begin to change. The waist and the derriere become more important. But by then you will be a *Maman* and your figure will be more full."

It was true that within ten years the waist would reappear and skirts become fuller, but it was obvious to Louise when she was handed up into the curricle that, fashion or no fashion, one of the narrow-skirted day dresses would be entirely unsuitable for such a venture. How would one step up so high without pulling one's skirt above the knee?

With her costume she wore a bonnet that, on the advice of Véronique, had a moderate poke with a matching lining and a jaunty but not extravagant feather.

"You do not wish your head to appear so large," she said. "Elegance, not extravagance!"

So it was that the Earl and Countess of Shrewsbury made their first appearance in the park as man and wife. Their happiness and enjoyment of each other's company made them unaware that they were receiving a number of curious glances, and several people who might have been expected to stop and exchange a few words simply rode by, looking the other way. The happy couple was too busy laughing at something one or the other had said to pay any attention to anyone else. In any case, the opinion of other people meant nothing to the Earl, and Louise was unaware of the habit of riders in the park stopping to talk with friends every few minutes.

Louise was down first after changing for dinner. It never took her long and Susan by now had the knack of doing her hair. She was sitting in the drawing room with a glass of sweet sherry when she heard the front doorbell ring and the Dowager Countess was shown in.

"My lady!" said Louise. "This is a pleasant surprise!"

"I think not, my dear, when you hear what I have to say, but we'll wait for Gareth."

Louise was taken aback, but before she could say anything, the Dowager continued. "And please call me Grandmother! We are members of the same family now. Let me say, you are positively blooming, Louise. May I conclude that all is now well between the two of you?"

"Yes, it is, but how did you know we were having… problems?"

"Oh, I'm an old lady, Louise, I've observed a lot of marriages. That whole story of your wagering the bracelet was just too silly. I knew that boy of mine must have done something to vex you. I rang a peal over him and told him to come and throw himself on your mercy. Did he do it?"

"Yes, well, I think it's fairer to say we threw ourselves on each other's mercy. I was as much to blame as he."

"Never admit such a thing, my dear! Let them think they are always in the wrong. Believe me, it's much easier that way. You talked when you first came to London about men always having the upper hand. But we have our own ways of getting what we want. It's best to learn that early. Ah, here he is!"

The Earl came in and as he kissed first his grandmother and then Louise on the cheek said, "How nice! My two favorite women waiting for me. I'm glad to see you, *Grandmother*. But what are you plotting?"

"Whatever can you mean? I never plot."

Gareth laughed. "Yes, and I never make an objection in the House of Lords! Come on now, Gran, out with it!"

"Don't call me that! Oh, thank you, Lisle." The butler had come in with his lordship's *fino* and a glass of *oloroso* for the Dowager. She waited until he left.

"It's those dratted caricatures. It's silly Betty Hightower, to whom I showed your picture of Caroline du Bois, you remember, Louise? Well, yesterday when those caricatures appeared in the newspaper, she told one of her bosom bows she'd seen one you had done just like it. By lunchtime today it was all over town that you are LS."

The Earl had just taken a sip of his sherry and spluttered, "What? What are you talking about? Louise is LS? Ridiculous! Just tell me who is spreading that tale about and I'll put a stop to it!"

Then he saw Louise's agonized expression and stopped.

"You don't mean it's true?"

The Dowager had put her hand to her mouth, her eyes wide.

"You didn't tell him?"

Dumbly, Louise shook her head. "N...no." She turned to her husband, "I... didn't want to vex you after we just... I didn't think there was any way they could be linked to me. I'd forgotten about Caroline du Bois."

She ran to him and fell at his knees. "I'm so sorry, Gareth. I'm so sorry."

"You mean you gave those pictures to the newspaper?" He was incredulous.

"No, of course not!"

And the whole story came out.

"You mean Rose, the maid you just asked me to send home in a carriage? In one of my carriages? I'll dismiss her first, and let her make her own way home! That's if I don't prosecute her for theft! Her and that newspaper boy!"

"No, darling, you can't do that. It wasn't her fault. She loved him!"

"Love!" The word exploded from his mouth.

There was total silence for a moment. Then the Dowager said, "Yes. Love. It can make you do the stupidest things. We all know that, don't we, Gareth?"

Chapter Fifty-Five

The Earl looked from his beloved grandmother to, as he had but recently realized, his equally beloved wife, and knew his grandmother was right. Love would make you do the stupidest things.

He stood up, raising his wife to her feet, and held her close.

"And just to think, I asked you earlier if you had any artistic talent!"

He kissed the top of her head.

"Stop crying, my dear. I can't afford another ruined waistcoat, not if you're going to order a gown embroidered with diamonds."

She looked up at him.

"Oh Gareth, I do so love you," she said, half-crying and half-laughing.

He kissed her on the lips.

"Good, that's settled," said the Dowager. "Now I'd better be going home."

"Not before dinner!" Louise, released herself from her husband's embrace and went to take her hands. "I'm sure Lisle has already had a place laid for you."

"Oh, my dear, I would definitely be *de trop*."

"You can never be *de trop* as far as I am concerned." Her grandson joined his wife. "I owe my happiness entirely to you. I remember complaining that women were so dull, but you found me the perfect match. She lectures me on women's equality, she gives away our jewels, she draws scurrilous pictures of us all and allows them to be published in the newspaper. There's never a dull moment. I have to go to the House to get some rest."

"And I owe my happiness to you too," agreed Louise. "You found me the perfect husband. He's rude, frowning and overbearing, but for some reason, I adore him."

The Dowager smiled lovingly at them both. "Very well then, but I shall leave directly after dinner. You two have things to do."

"What things?" asked Louise before she could stop herself.

Her husband raised his eyebrows. She blushed and the Dowager laughed.

Lisle chose that moment to come in and announce, "Dinner is served, my lady."

The following morning the Earl left the house soon after breakfast on some mysterious mission of his own which he vouchsafed to no one.

Then the couple spent the afternoon playing cards in the garden sitting room with the doors open and the sounds of summer reaching their ears. Louise confessed she had misled her husband about her card playing.

"You see, I didn't want to play as your partner that first time. I was very upset with you and I was hoping you'd choose to play with someone else."

"Well," responded her husband, shuffling expertly. "You'd better do your best now. I warn you, I have some interesting ideas for penalties if you lose, and they're nothing to do with vowels or bracelets."

That evening they were invited to the last party of the season at the home of the Duke and Duchess of Avondale. This was a not-to-be-missed event every year and all the best and brightest would be there. They had accepted weeks ago, and the Earl was determined to go. Louise begged her husband to allow her to send excuses.

"We can't possibly go!" she cried. "Everyone will snub us. It will be dreadful. Oh, please, Gareth, can't we stay quietly at home?"

"By no means," he said firmly. "We are going. Put on your best bib and tucker. Wear all the diamonds."

"Even the necklace?" Louise gulped.

"Yes."

"I shall look like a turkey."

"I like turkeys." He kissed her. "Do as I ask, my love. It will be fine. You'll see."

So Louise arrayed herself in yet another new gown. This was of grey-blue silk, exactly the color of her eyes. Her bosom and narrow waist were enhanced by an insert of ivory lace over the silk in the bodice. Otherwise, the gown was perfectly plain. She wore matching ivory lace gloves, the bracelet, and the drop earrings, but was in despair about what to do with the necklace. It looked dreadful with the V neck of the gown and felt as if it were strangling her. Then Susan suggested wearing it around the curls on the top of her head.

"You've got a lot of hair, m'lady," she said. "I know I can fasten it so it don't slip."

They tried it and it looked very regal. Louise's abundant and springy hair held up the ponderous piece.

"I'll have to make sure his lordship approves of my wearing a necklace on my head," said Louise, "but it does solve the problem. Thank you, Susan."

Her husband's reaction was characteristic. "I don't care if you wear it as a belt," he said, kissing her. "But it looks very nice like that. Perhaps we don't need to alter it after all."

"Especially if the next Countess has the neck of a swan," said Louise.

"Or a boa constrictor," added her husband.

Chapter Fifty-Six

They arrived a little late at the Avondale mansion because the Earl had suddenly remembered something he had to do before they left. Louise was a bundle of nerves when they walked into the noble couple's drawing room. It was completely full. A total hush fell on the assembled company and people stepped back as they advanced. When they reached the center of the room they stood alone, all eyes upon them.

The Earl took Louise's hand. "Head up," he whispered. "Let them see the necklace."

Then he spoke in a carrying voice that must have been, Louise thought, the one he used to quell any objections in the House of Lords.

"Good evening, my friends. It is fortuitous that we find so many of you here tonight, as my wife and I have an announcement to make. You will all have seen the publication earlier this week of a number of unflattering images of some of you. As you know, I myself did not escape."

There was a loud murmur at this.

"By now you are aware that my wife was the artist responsible. If you are like me, you will admire her talent while deploring her choice of subject matter. We deeply regret that you should have seen them."

Another loud murmur.

"Let me say at once the portraits were not intended for publication. My wife did them for her own amusement when she first arrived in London and was practically without acquaintance. She barely knew any of the persons represented. Unfortunately, the images were removed without permission from my wife's possession and published without her knowledge."

Interested murmurs.

"That doesn't, of course, make the shock of them any the less for those who came under her critical eye. It is never pleasant to see ourselves as others see us. But none of us whose image was thus displayed can deny that the characteristics they show were accurate. We are what we are, and as such we provide amusement for each other. The novelist Miss Austen put it best a couple of years ago: *For what do we live but to make sport for our neighbors and laugh at them in our turn?*"

A few nods, a shadow of laughter.

"I have taken steps to make sure the images do not reappear, but we will understand if you chose henceforth to eschew our company. We will regret the friendly communication with you we once had, and will be the poorer for the lack of it, but we will have to consider ourselves well served. Now, if you wish to turn away, that is your prerogative. We will wait for you to make the first step."

Gareth squeezed her hand again as they stood together in the ensuing silence.

It did not last long. People began to come up to them; they bowed, curtseyed, shook his lordship's hand, and a few of the ladies even whispered, "How do you do it, my dear? How clever you are! Do you have any more?" Louise smiled and shook her head. Very few of the company turned away.

After a while, the crowd separated them. Louise was glad to seek a quieter corner of the room but had only been there a moment when she was aware of a familiar figure making its way towards her.

"My lady," Diane Courtland curtseyed. "I'm happy to have a brief opportunity to talk to you. I have to confess to entirely underestimating you. Now I wish we had known each other before... before all this. I think we could have been friends."

"I'm sorry if I hurt you," Louise deciding to be equally frank. "I was just so jealous."

"You had no need to be, you know. He never came near me after you were married."

"I know that now. I didn't then."

"Men are such silly creatures. He told me marriage would make no difference to us, and I think he honestly believed it. But when it came to it, something prevented him. He said it was because of Youngbrough, and perhaps for a moment it was. But he knew I would drop Denis in an instant. No, he could have come to me, but he didn't. It was honor probably. Or upbringing. You know, those nannies form more of their character than most people realize. His must have made him believe fidelity is more important than pleasure."

"But he does have pleasure... with me."

"I'm glad to hear it. I hope you do, too."

"Oh, yes!"

"Then we are alike. I thought so."

She smiled. "I don't suppose we shall speak again. But I want you to know: you won and I admire you for it."

Then Diane Courtland curtseyed and was gone.

She had won. Louise never thought of it like that before. She, plain, unremarkable Louise Grey. She had won. She went back to rejoin her husband with a spring in her step.

On the way home in the carriage, Louise took her husband's hand. "You are wonderful, you know. I've just realized why you made sure we were a little late. You wanted everyone to be there. Why didn't you tell me what you were going to do?"

"Husbands can have secrets too, you know."

"Oh, let's not have any more! Let's tell each other everything!"

"I can't guarantee that. There may be things you're best not knowing."

"If you're thinking I wouldn't know if you took a mistress, I should and it would be the worse for you. The incident of the bracelet...."

"And the caricatures," added her husband,

"And the caricatures...," agreed his wife, "would be nothing compared with what I should do."

"I believe you. But you may be sure that whatever secret I keep, it won't be that."

Louise thought about what Diane had said and smiled to herself.

Then she asked, "But what was that you said about taking steps to make sure the images don't reappear?"

"I went to see the publishers this morning and persuaded them."

"How? Did you pay them a great deal of money?"

"Ah, that's one of the secrets I'm keeping."

Chapter Fifty-Seven

That morning the Earl had paid a visit to *The Times* publishing house.

"My name is Shrewsbury," he said, on being introduced into the offices of John Walter, the editor. "You are going to give me the blocks used to print the illustrations of the caricatures you recently published, together with the original sketches, which are, in fact, property stolen from my home. I could sue you for publishing material to which you had no right. But because I recognize the commercial loss to you, I am prepared to pay you five hundred pounds."

The publisher made a sound of dissent, but the Earl held up his hand.

"The tax on newspapers is fourpence and you sell yours for sixpence," he continued. "You therefore receive twopence per paper. I am offering you the value of sixty thousand newspapers. I am reliably informed your circulation is five thousand a day. That is twelve days of circulation. You will correct me if I am mistaken. We all know the term *a nine-day wonder*. These caricatures are no more than that. You will come out ahead."

"But my dear Lord Shrewsbury!" replied the editor, "Much as it pains me to say it, they are not for sale. We are entertaining offers to make them into a book."

"It will pain you a great deal more if you don't immediately hand them over."

"What do you mean?"

"I shall find the woodblocks which are no doubt on the premises and break them over your head." The Earl spoke quite calmly.

Looking at his powerful physique, the editor did not doubt he could do it. But he was a courageous man.

"You would not dare!"

"Do you place your faith in that? You are mistaken. Consider my position: I am a man seeking to protect the honor of his wife. I am the victim of a theft from which you have profited. I have made you a good faith monetary offer. What court would blame me if in the heat of passion I subject you to injury?"

Mr. Walter could see he was beaten. He knew the Shrewsbury name. He knew his lordship had the ear of the most powerful people in the land. His father had run afoul of the aristocracy often enough, and had ended up twice in Newgate. The son had no desire to follow suit, nor, it must be said, to have his head broken. Besides, he had not known the caricatures were stolen.

"Very well," he conceded. "Give me the money and I'll have my people bring up the woodblocks."

"You will forgive my natural skepticism, but I prefer to see them where they lie. Who is to say if, in the confusion of the moment, one or other of them might be forgotten?"

Grumbling, the editor led his lordship to a downstairs chamber where a number of men were sitting around a large table, busily engraving on quite small pieces of wood. Gareth's curiosity overcame him.

"Surely these blocks aren't big enough for images the size of those you publish?"

"No," agreed the editor. "We put several together. We have to use boxwood, you see, because it holds up to the presses better than any other wood. But it has to be cut across the grain, and the pieces don't come very big. We have to have several artists working on one illustration. They each do a section. We lock it together after. Anyway, your blocks and the originals are over there."

He gestured to a pile standing on a side table. The Earl counted them. He knew how many images had been published. They were all there. In a folder next to them sat Louise's drawings. He picked them up.

A few minutes later the business was accomplished. The woodblocks were in his lordship's carriage and the five hundred pounds were in the editor's pocket.

The Earl extended his hand, "Thank you," he said. "I'm glad I didn't have to break your head. I like you."

"I wish I could say the same," replied John Walter, but he took the proffered hand.

His lordship laughed and left him.

The editor then went immediately to the reporters' pool and spoke to the man who had bought the caricatures from Freddy.

"You want to be more careful where you get stuff from, my lad," he said. "Those caricatures were stolen. We could've been in a lot of trouble. I've sorted it out, but if it happens again, it'll be your job."

The next time Freddy put in an appearance, the reporter told him to push off. "Nearly cost me my job, you did," he said. "I'm not taking another tip from you, and neither will anyone else if I know anything about it."

So Freddy never did make the money he dreamed of. He continued to deliver newspapers and charm the kitchen maids until he was finally forced to marry one. She wasn't as scrupulous about the ring on her finger as Rose had been, and enjoyed the pleasures of marriage before the event, with the inevitable consequences. He quickly forgot Rose, but then, to do her credit, she just as quickly forgot him.

When the Earl got home he jumped out of the carriage and prepared to go inside.

"What shall we do with them wooden things, my lord?" asked the groom who had leaped down to pull out the unnecessary steps.

"Burn 'em. All of them. Nothing but ashes, you hear?"

The groom nodded and did as he had been told. He made a bonfire and was amazed how long it lasted. The lads in the stables baked themselves a few potatoes in the ashes.

"That were some good wood," they agreed.

Chapter Fifty-Eight

After the party at Avondale House, it seemed no time at all before the Earl and Countess of Shrewsbury removed to the country for the summer. They were both glad to get out of London. Afterwards, they would both remember their time at Overshott as halcyon days. Louise loved the country home, with its lack of formality, the comfortable old furniture, its early dinnertime, and the long evenings to walk and talk with her husband. She loved the gardens, the hothouses, the home farm, the burgeoning wildlife, the old flowering bushes, the cats and the dogs.

Towards the end of August she began to feel sick in the mornings, her breasts were swollen and tender and she was grateful that the prevailing style was for dresses with no waist.

By the time they returned to London for the opening of the House in October, her pregnancy was past the initial phase. She felt extraordinarily well. Her sallow coloring was replaced by a pink bloom in her cheek and her hair, always abundant, shone like a bird's wing. She commented on her improved appearance to her husband and his reply was characteristic.

"We'll just have to keep you increasing all the time. I promise to work especially hard on that."

The *ton* of course, wondered how the infant would turn out. The Earl was annoyed when he found out there were wagers in the clubs that her ladyship would give birth to a daughter with eyebrows like her Papa, but that was another secret he kept from his wife.

In the event, Louise gave birth to a boy who looked remarkably like his grandmother, the pretty blond lady whose portrait hung on the family dining room wall. But if his appearance was sweet, his character seemed quite the opposite. He filled the Shrewsbury townhouse with his strident demands for sustenance every two hours, day and night. He was only happy so long as he was being fed. Louise did not want to employ a wet nurse, but after a particularly difficult night she was so exhausted she was considering it.

"Give him porridge!" suggested her husband. "That's what they gave me in China. I remember my mother saying I was constantly hungry when I was a baby and oats were one thing they recognized from back home. They boiled it up with milk and shoveled into me. Look at the result." He beat his broad chest.

"I suppose it's worth a try," said Louise, smiling tiredly. "Just a little, if we cut the oats up very fine and boil them well."

This program was put into operation and the gods smiled on them. Young Christopher (he was named for his grandfather) ate as much as they would give him, then his mother nursed him asleep. He slept six hours. The household breathed a collective sigh of relief.

After that, he grew like an oak. It was obvious he was going to be just like his Papa, without the eyebrows. Then it became apparent that in spite of his angelic face, he had his Papa's character, too. He was fiercely uncompromising. His favorite word was "No!"

But then Louise presented her husband with another son. He had his father's nose and heavy brow and looked like a monkey when he was a baby. He was never handsome, but he overcame the burden of his eyebrows by being a smiling, amenable boy.

Everyone loved him. He was as conciliating as his brother was argumentative. As they grew older, they were a perfect foil for each other and formed an unbreakable bond.

Finally Louise had a longed-for daughter, who turned into such a beautiful young woman her Papa said he should put her into a castle with a high wall and a moat to keep the suitors away. Christopher volunteered to patrol the perimeter. But since from the very first her mother had inculcated her with ideas of women's equality, the lovely girl stoutly declared she was well able to look after herself. She certainly ruled the roost over both her brothers and her besotted father.

Motherhood suited Louise. From the moment her first suckling infant put his tiny hand up to her face and smiled at her around her nipple, she knew here was someone who would never think her plain. She was right. Her children thought her the most wonderful person in the world. Her drawings made them laugh, and when she accompanied them with comic voices matching the character, they rolled on the floor, crying, "More, Mama! More!"

Lady Esmé did get to hold all her great-grandchildren. She was immensely proud of them. According to her, they were the best-looking family in London.

"I knew you could do it," she said to Gareth when she was a very old lady.

"Not without you, Gran," he replied.

Out of habit she began to protest his use of the name she so disliked, but since, with the encouragement of their father, her great-grandchildren all called her Gran-Gran, she smiled.

"Very well. I give up. Gran it is."

"It always was," he said.

The End

Note from the Author

If you enjoyed this novel, please leave a review! Go to the Amazon page and scroll down past all the other books Amazon wants you to buy(!) till you get to the review click. Thank you so much!

Here is the page link: A Marriage is Arranged

Or you can use this QR code:

For a free short story and to listen to the author read the first chapter of all her novels, please go to the website:

https://romancenovelsbyglrobinson.com

Here's a preview of my next novel, **Repairing A Broken Heart**, now on pre-order. It's due out just before Valentine's Day 2024. Please consider pre-ordering it! This is the link:

Chapter One of *Repairing a Broken Heart*

"I absolutely refuse to marry Malcom Foxworthy." Lyla confronted her father in the library, whither she had been summoned. "I don't love him. In fact I don't even like him."

Her father's would have torn his hair had it not been carefully pomaded to cover an unfortunate thinning over the top.

"Is that all you've got to say?" Anger suffused his face. "I shelled out the blunt for a London season to get you safely settled and you had several advantageous offers, all of which you refused. If you're holding out for young Blankley, let me tell you, you're wasting your time. Now he's back from his travels I hear he's been seeing a lot of Daphne Warner. She's got a sight deal more to offer than you have. I daresay she don't know as much about horses as you do, but she has twenty thousand a year. For Blankley Senior that's a good deal more to the purpose than being able to mix a poultice, I can tell you. Everyone's saying they're only just staying ahead of the bailiffs."

He stood in front of the mirror. He was used to being thought a good-looking man and was vain of his appearance. Now his high color showed not only on his face but up in his scalp, barely covered by his thinning hair. That distressed him more than his daughter. He took a deep breath and patted his coiffure, trying to regain his composure.

"I blame your mother," he said at last. "If she hadn't upped and died like that, you'd have had someone to get you ready for a man instead of spending all your time in the stables."

"It wasn't poor Mama's fault she contracted a fever! And anyway, I don't think it would have made any difference. I never could learn to sew, or draw, or play the pianoforte. All those governesses tried their best but it was no use. The only thing I'm good at is dealing with horses. And you know that's a good thing, Papa. You've got to admit I'm helpful there."

"That's as may be. But the stables ain't going to help you get a husband, Lyla! You're good-looking, like everyone on my side of the family, and there's no denying you'd make any man a cozy armful." He caught sight of himself again in the large gilt mirror over the fireplace and preened, thrusting his shoulders back. "But no one's going to be looking for you in the stalls with the horses. No one except young Blankley and as I said, he's spoken for. He's marrying Daphne Warner."

"He can't be! Who is Daphne Warner? I know no one by that name! Harry has never mentioned her! He and I have an... an understanding, Papa. He told me his family needs money. He knows Mama didn't leave me very much. Our stables do well, but not enough to give the Blankleys what they need."

"They certainly don't! Anyway, as I said, it all arranged. Whether you know her or not, he's to marry the Warner girl."

"You must be mistaken, Papa, really. He has a plan! He told me he was going to India to take up some business or the other and make enough money to send home. Then in three or four years when he's cleared the debts, he'll come home to marry me. I said I'd wait."

"Three or four years? Are you mad? If the bailiffs are at the gate they don't have three or four weeks!"

"But Harry said..."

"Listen to me, my girl. I don't care what Harry said. He'll do his duty by his family and if it means marrying the Warner girl, that's what he'll do."

"I don't believe it!" Lyla brushed angry tears from her eyes. "I'm going there right now to ask him myself."

It was a testimony to his daughter's independent ways that her father found nothing remarkable in this announcement. He was used to her going off where and when she liked. He never worried that she might get into trouble and barely remembered the one time when she had. She was about twelve and hadn't come back by dinner time. He might not have noticed that either had her maid Potter not come to him, worried that Miss Lyla hadn't come home and it was getting dark. He'd been persuaded to send out a search party and they'd found her lying in a ditch with her horse next to her.

"It wasn't Bobby's fault," she said, "He didn't see the dip and neither did I. It wasn't there before. All that rain must have opened it up. He's got sprained fetlock. I ripped up my petticoat and bandaged him with wet strips, but they'll need taking off soon or they'll do more harm than good. Put a splint on him with some dry ones and try to get him up. I'll do a fomentation when we get back to the stable."

"But Miss Lyla!" said Jeb, a stable lad who admired her and had set out to find her the minute she was reported missing. They were much the same age. "Your ankle! Is it broken? It looks awful bad!"

"I don't know. Probably. But don't worry about me. It's just that I couldn't stand up to deal with Bobby."

Needless to say, this story had gone around the village in a flash. Young Miss Lyla hadn't cried when they set her ankle (it *had* been broken). All she did was ask about her horse and if they hadn't stopped her, she would have been in the stable day and night to look after it. The boys all thought she was a real goer and any girl criticizing her was called a jealous cat.

This is the link to pre-order, or you may use the QR code at the top of the preview.

Repairing a Broken Heart

Thank you!

Other Novels by GL Robinson

Please go to my Amazon Author Page for more information:

GLRobinson-US

GLRobinson-UK

Or my website: https://romancenovelsbyglrobinsoncom

About The Author

GL Robinson is a retired French professor who started writing Regency Romances in 2018. She dedicates all her Regency novels to her sister, who died unexpectedly that year and who, like her, had a lifelong love of the genre. She remembers the two of them reading Georgette Heyer after lights out under the covers in their convent boarding school and giggling together in delicious complicity.

Brought up in the south of England, she has spent the last forty years in upstate New York with her American husband. She likes gardening, talking with her grandchildren and sitting by the fire. She still reads Georgette Heyer.

Printed in Great Britain
by Amazon